200+ WAYS TO
PROTECT
— 🔒 — YOUR — 🔒 —
PRIVACY

Simple Ways to Prevent Hacks and Protect Your Privacy—On and Offline

JENI ROGERS

ADAMS MEDIA
NEW YORK   LONDON   TORONTO   SYDNEY   NEW DELHI

Adams Media
An Imprint of Simon & Schuster, Inc.
57 Littlefield Street
Avon, Massachusetts 02322

First Adams Media trade paperback edition January 2019

ADAMS MEDIA and colophon are trademarks of Simon & Schuster.

For information about special discounts for bulk purchases, please contact Simon & Schuster Special Sales at 1-866-506-1949 or business@simonandschuster.com.

The Simon & Schuster Speakers Bureau can bring authors to your live event. For more information or to book an event contact the Simon & Schuster Speakers Bureau at 1-866-248-3049 or visit our website at www.simonspeakers.com.

Interior design by Sylvia McArdle
Interior images © Getty Images

Manufactured in the United States of America

10 9 8 7 6 5 4 3 2 1

Library of Congress Cataloging-in-Publication Data has been applied for.

ISBN 978-1-72140-012-6
ISBN 978-1-72140-013-3 (ebook)

Dedication

To my family and My Love, thank you for supporting my dreams, however whimsical. To my sweet son who always restores my belief in super powers and focuses my gaze to the wonder in life. And to everyone who believes in the good and stands alongside me to preserve it in this world...this is for you too.

Contents

CHAPTER **1**

Protecting Your Offline Privacy—at Home, in Public, and Everywhere In-Between 16

CHAPTER **2**

Protecting the Privacy of Your Children (and Teaching Them to Protect Themselves) . . 60

CHAPTER **3**

Strategies for Protecting Yourself and Your Private Data on Mobile Devices 89

CHAPTER **4**

Strategies and Best Practices for Staying Safe and Protecting Your Privacy Online . . . 127

CHAPTER **5**

How to Enjoy Social Media While
Retaining Your Privacy **163**

CHAPTER **6**

Strategies for Protecting Yourself and Your Privacy in Email, Online Classifieds, and Online Dating 193

Introduction

Privacy and confidentiality are in the news these days as social media, credit monitoring, and big businesses have suffered massive data breaches—despite their promises to protect our information.

The Internet isn't the only place where your privacy can be invaded. Your home, your photos, your trash can, your kids, your favorite restaurant or store—and even *you*—can provide your private information to everyone from thieves to busybodies. What once was considered private information is now widely shared not just on social media and websites, but from person to person. Protecting your personal information in today's world is essential.

In this book, you'll find more than two hundred hacks to help you understand the everyday things you may be doing that put you at risk. It'll also show you how to limit the access to your personal information and life and make it more secure from scammers and hackers. Just remember: you may have scruples and morals, but others don't. These privacy protection hacks will help you shift your thinking and give you more control over the loopholes, workarounds, and threats that lurk on the edges of your most sensitive data.

You'll find hacks that will show you how to keep your documents confidential, how to safely download and use apps, how to choose appropriate and safe passwords, and how to protect your privacy when you're traveling. You'll be able to sleep in comfort knowing that you and your family are safe from malicious hackers and cyber-thieves.

The best news is that you don't need to hire a specialist or mistrust everyone to keep your information safe—you can protect yourself with some simple steps. All you need is this book's easy-to-implement privacy protection hacks.

CHAPTER 1

Protecting Your Offline Privacy—at Home, in Public, and Everywhere In-Between

Protecting your privacy isn't just about adjusting your on-line account settings or properly using passwords. This isn't to say these things aren't important, because they are vital to fully protecting your privacy. However, securing your private information starts much closer to home. In fact, much of it starts in your home and revolves around the personal data you use each day as an extension of your home and family life. A large portion of your life takes place inside your home. You live there, share meals with your family, create memories, and relax in a place that's like a safe hideaway.

However, your personal data and private information also live in your home…in drawers and file cabinets, on the counter, in stacks on your desk, or even in your trash can. Like you, your data doesn't just stay at home either. As you go about your day, it comes along with you. You carry personal data from home to work in your purse or wallet and on your cell phone. You take it to the coffee shop for a meeting, you set it on the table during lunch, you may leave it in your car to run into the store for just a couple of things.

These privacy protection hacks will help you understand the important (but simple) ways you can protect yourself and your personal data at home, in public, and everywhere in-between.

Hang On to Your Privacy
by "The Shred"

Bank and credit card statements, medical bills or paperwork, insurance documents...these items may seem like harmless pieces of paper stacked on a table or crammed in a drawer, but they can each contain private information about you: your birthdate, bank account numbers, credit card accounts, or even your social security number.

You should shred any paperwork that contains your private details. While it may seem like an unnecessary step (I mean, why not just throw them away?) the reality is that there are crooks out there who aren't above rifling through trash bins to look for bits of your private life and data that they can use maliciously. Shredding documents containing sensitive data is really quite easy, and for some, very satisfying! Make sure to empty your shredder across a few different garbage bags before disposing of them.

Shut Off the Junk Mail
Data Siphon

"You're preapproved for a $1 million loan! Funds tomorrow!"
"Refinance your car loan! Prequalification code inside."

If you're like many people, you probably understand this mail isn't offering you anything valuable, and you likely just toss it in the trash without a second thought (and maybe, a scoff). But you need to take this a couple steps further to ensure that private data belonging to you does not get into the wrong hands.

- Don't leave these items in your mailbox or throw them into the trash intact.
- These pre-qualifications and other loan offers contain codes that could be tracked to you and your credit card accounts, so it's important that you shred these types of offers before you dispose of them.
- But before you do, try to find contact information on the offers and call or write them to let them know you prohibit them to send you this type of mail.

Turn off the junk mail data siphon, and then shred. Shred without mercy.

Watch Out for Falsely Requested Personal Data via Phone

Never—and I mean never!—give out your personal data to someone who calls you saying there's a payment problem (if you're at a hotel, go down to the front desk; if it's about a company, call the company, etc.).

Let's look at an example, based on a true story of a phone hack that swindled unassuming hotel guests.

You're staying in a hotel. You've checked in, gotten your key-cards, and are getting settled, unpacking, dancing in the luxurious bathrobe the hotel provides. Suddenly the phone in your hotel room rings. You answer, and the caller identifies herself as the hotel manager, and then goes on to tell you there's been an issue with your credit card and she needs to run it again.

This should raise a red flag.

If anything ever happens that makes you say, "Hmmm, that's weird..." trust that instinct and seek out someone to help you. In this example, you should go down to the front desk and sort out the issue (if there is one) in person, face-to-face with the hotel manager.

That's how you should handle any scenario where a person you don't know (but claims to be in authority) asks for personal data over the phone. Go directly to the source and never provide your credit card (other personal data) via phone, no matter who that person claims to be.

Protect Your Payment Details When You Order Delivery Food

Many of your favorite restaurants probably offer the option to have your meals prepared and delivered fresh and hot to your door. While this is a great convenience, you should take care not to move from "convenient" to "lazy" when it comes to placing your delivery order, particularly if you're making your order over the phone.

- Never provide your credit card number, expiration date, and security PIN over the phone when ordering delivery food. If you pass along your payment information over the phone, you're putting it in the hands of the person who takes your call, who then hands it off to the delivery driver on your receipt.
- Only use your debit or credit card to order in if a restaurant you trust offers a secure online payment option through their website or app.
- Otherwise (or if you're trying out a new place you've never ordered from before) just use cash.

Don't Fax Private Documents

Truthfully, it's probably a good idea to avoid faxing any documents at all, no matter the nature of the content. This technology is quickly becoming outdated, and most fax machines are not updated with the modern security features you need when you share documents. There are much safer and more convenient ways to safely send documents (such as sending a scan right to your email address).

You never really know who will have access to that document once you've faxed it over. Someone other than the person whom you intended to share it with may get it into his hands, and those hands may be itching with malicious intent.

If you must fax something, never fax documents that contain private details such as your address, social security number, credit card details, insurance information, or medical records.

Lock Up Your Private Paper Documents

Social security cards, birth certificates, and tax returns all contain some of your most sensitive information, and they're also all paper documents. It's vital you keep them stored safely in your home so that you know where they are when you need them and that they're secure in the event your home security is ever compromised. Burglars not only go for valuables but will also often try to grab paperwork or files that will help them in their evil pursuit of identity theft.

- Keep all of your important paper documents stored in a safe and secure place like a locked desk drawer or a personal safe.
- Make sure your safe is not in plain sight.
- Use a fireproof box to further protect your personal documents.

Only Carry the Necessities

You probably carry around a lot of personal data each day that you don't really need, so stick to the basics and only take necessities with you each time you venture out into the world, such as:

- ID
- Keys
- Phone
- Wallet or purse (holding just your ID and one card you need—not all of them)

Monitoring and limiting what personal information you pack will also limit what other people can get hold of as you cross paths all day long, but you should make a special point never to regularly carry around sensitive documents (such as your social security card or birth certificate) on your person.

Keep Your Personal Items Close (and Your Personal Data Closer)

When you're out in a public place, always keep your personal items on your person. Leaving your purse in the shopping cart while you pick the best produce may seem okay because it just takes a minute, but the truth is that thieves troll places where someone might leave her personal items unattended due to distractions, even if they last only for a few seconds.

Keeping your personal items safe is important at home as well. Don't leave your keys or purse close to the door or in plain sight from your windows. This could give a lurking thief the motivation and the means to steal your items. Much like in public places, it could happen faster than you'd ever think.

Lock Up Your Personal Items at Work

Your personal items can give away a lot of private information you wouldn't want a coworker to know, especially if she has bad intentions. As a general rule, you should not take private materials to work with you, but for the everyday items you need (but also want secure) you should:

- Put your personal items in a locked drawer in your desk.
- Secure your private items in a locker that only you have the key or combination to. Otherwise secure your personal items so that they are safe from the prying eyes that could be looking around your workplace.

Require a Signature on Your Package Deliveries

One of the easiest ways you can avoid giving away private information that may be on or inside the packages that come to your home is to require a signature for the package to be delivered. If no one is available to sign for the package when it arrives, it will be taken back to the mail facility, where you can pick it up yourself and ensure that it doesn't sit unattended on your porch. A package sitting in plain sight on your porch or front steps can tempt passersby to sneak a peek at your private details or go so far as to sneak away with your package.

Protect Your Packages by Scheduling Deliveries

You aren't going to be home every time your packages are delivered. Those with a thieving, devious spirit have begun capitalizing on this more and more of late, particularly around holidays when you'll usually have more packages being delivered.

A great way to ensure that your packages are not stolen when you aren't home is to schedule your deliveries for a time of day you know someone *will* be home. Once you receive your confirmation number, call the mail service that will be delivering your package and set up a time to have your package delivered.

Use Multiple Addresses
(and Do It Strategically)

Your credit and debit cards must be tied to a billing address to ensure you receive statements, bills, and notifications via mail. When you place orders online, you'll also have to provide a shipping address, which if you're ordering something for yourself or someone in your household, will be the same as your billing address.

The risk here is that when all your addresses are the same, someone getting hold of one means he knows them all. You can maintain much more anonymity online if you use different addresses for different purposes. Keep your home address private and set up a P.O. Box or a "real street address" where you can receive mail and packages at a designated facility where you go pick them up. Using different addresses, particularly in your online shopping activities, can help shield your actual address without losing the great conveniences of shopping online.

Have New Checks Mailed to Your Alternate Address

If you still use checks, you should consider using more updated and secure forms of payment. However, you may still need to use checks infrequently for paying your rent or setting up direct deposit payment with your new employer. Let's take a quick look at everything one single check (even a voided one) can give away about your personal life:

- Your name
- Your address
- Your phone number
- Your driver's license number
- Your bank account and routing numbers

In the wrong hands, all these tidbits combined could put your privacy (and your finances) in serious jeopardy. So if you must use checks, have them sent to one of your alternate addresses where you have to go and physically pick up your mail. You don't want that level of personal information just sitting in your mailbox.

Put Your Mail On Hold During Vacations or Family Trips

Whether you're leaving for a family vacation or will be out of town for a long trip of any kind, you will most certainly lock your home up when you leave. But what about your mailbox? While you're away, your mail will pile up in that box, and most of it could contain personal details that will be easily accessible to busybodies or thieves who may be prowling around your neighborhood. If you're going to be gone for a long trip, make sure you contact your postal service and put a vacation hold on your mail. There may be a small fee to pause your mail, but it's well worth it to keep your personal information secure until you're home to collect your mail and shred the items you don't need.

Take Your Outgoing Mail to the Post Office

That cute little red flag signaling outgoing mail in your mailbox is like a beacon for cons and crooks (who aren't above sifting through your mail to try and find money or personal information about you in its contents). Whenever you have outgoing mail, particularly if you're mailing bills or anything containing private information, make a trip to the post office. You can send the item from their secured mailboxes and avoid turning on that red beacon alerting crooks you have outgoing mail.

Never Provide Your Social Security Number or Driver's License Number on a Hand-Written Form

Although it's becoming much less common in our digital era, there may still be times when you're required to fill out a form or application by hand, with a pen. (Don't worry, you'll never have to do it in cursive.) While physical forms are often still necessary in many situations, they're problematic when it comes to protecting your privacy. Once you fill out the form and hand it over, you have no insight into how it is stored or whose hands touch it. Anytime you relinquish control of a form containing your information, you're giving up your rights to your privacy. And you don't have to.

Never give out your social security number, driver's license number, or other sensitive information on a hand-written form you'll never see again. If you're in a position where you're forced to write down such details, that's a bad omen and you're well within your rights to refuse.

Avoid the Free T-Shirt

"Sign up today and get a free T-shirt that doubles as a shot glass!"
"Apply Today For 10% Off! No Approval Necessary!"

Free stuff is enticing. But the thing is, nothing is ever *truly* free.

When you provide your private information to the booth or store on a form or (even more shockingly) aloud, there is a risk that your personal data will be lost or get into fraudulent hands. "Free" doesn't seem like such a great deal anymore, does it?

Avoid signing up for a credit card or retail store card at a booth or in the store. If you are interested in obtaining a card, visit the bank that issues the card or go to the website for the retail establishment where you can apply through the highly secure and regulated channels offered there.

Don't Put Your Key under the Mat...Hide It Better Than That

To be prepared for those times you'll inevitably lock yourself out, it is certainly a good idea to have a spare key accessible somewhere outside the house so that you can let yourself back in. Many families put a key under the doormat or under a planter close to the door because these places are convenient. But these spots have become so ubiquitous as key "hiding" zones that they'll also be the very first places a thief will check if he's trying to gain entry to your home and all the private information inside. So, hide a key, but be clever and think outside the box, or the doormat, or the planter. Find a location that's uncommon and that no one would ever look (or be able to easily find) unless they know exactly where to look.

Properly Dispose of Prescription Medication Bottles

Have you ever given your prescription medication bottles a really thorough read? Aside from glancing at the name of the medicine and the instructions for how you should safely take it, you may not have given too much thought to all the personal details that the label holds:

- Your name
- Your address
- Your phone number
- Your health plan information

That's quite a bit of private information, isn't it? This is why you should make sure that you always properly dispose of your prescription medication bottles. Destroy the label containing all your private information before you throw the empty bottle in the garbage. Peel it off and shred it to make sure that a trash sifter isn't able to get your personal details and health information from garbage.

Don't Keep Private Documents at Work

You can never be too careful when it comes to what information you bring to your office or other places of work. You should always limit the private information that comes with you to work, and always leave private things at home, secured. These include:

- Mail containing private information
- Bank or credit card statements
- Birth certificate
- Social security card

Even if you have a locked file system at work, keep your private documents out of it. Instead, secure them in your home where they belong.

Go Green (for Your Privacy and the Planet) with Paperless Bills and Statements

Your mailbox is like a petri dish for privacy invasions. Every day you probably receive mail that contains personal information regarding your finances, health, or other private matters—and it just sits in your mailbox until you come home and take your envelopes and papers inside.

You should:

- Check your mail every day.
- Safely file or shred any paperwork that you do not need to keep.
- Better yet, turn on paperless billing for your banking statements, bills, notifications, etc. so that no paperwork festers in your mailbox and attracts snoops who are looking for an identity to steal or a credit card to fund an unauthorized purchase. Protect your privacy and save some trees? Win-win!

Monitor Your Bank Statement for Unrecognized Purchases (Large and Tiny)

If your credit card or bank account information has been breached, the first thing that these savvy crooks with no scruples will do is send through a charge for a very small amount, most times just a couple of cents. It's an amount you'd probably never notice, which is what they count on to validate your stolen card data and prepare for a larger and much more financially devastating move by making a large purchase.

Follow these tips:

- Check your transactions log in your online banking or credit statements often.
- Keep an eye out for these minute charges, which can lead to privacy breaching and money stealing.
- If you see a very small charge, notify your bank or credit institution immediately so they can flag the transaction, research it, and block any further charges.

Be Smarter Than Your Smart Home Devices

While smart home devices are very convenient, they can also generate privacy risks for you and your family. You can avoid these risks by taking the proper steps to secure your smart devices and staying smart in how you use them. Here's a quick overview that applies to all smart devices, and how you can ensure you stay smarter than they are.

- Use strong passwords for your devices, and change them frequently. (Use two-factor authentication wherever available. This extra security option requires not only a password but also entering a code sent to a separate device that only you should be able to access.)
- Change any default settings, codes, or passwords that come loaded on the device. Alter them to ones unique to you.
- Turn off or disable any smart device features you are not using.
- Turn off smart devices and disconnect them from Wi-Fi when you're not using them.
- Protect your Wi-Fi with a strong password and disable guest access.
- Consider setting up a separate Wi-Fi network specifically for your smart devices to add an extra layer of protection for your personal information.

Now we'll move into the specifics of how to outsmart your individual smart devices!

Stay Savvy in the Smart Speaker Craze

While smart speakers can add a tremendous amount of convenience (as well as fun and novelty) into your life and home, they can also provide a portal for hackers to gain entry and listen in on your home or even access other devices you have tethered to this device via Wi-Fi or Bluetooth.

Enjoy your smart speaker, but also take great care with whom you're inadvertently inviting into your home in the name of convenience. Follow these easy tips:

- Do not use the default commands programmed into the speaker. Train the speaker to recognize and respond only to the voices in your household.
- Create custom commands for your smart speaker that are meaningful only to you and your family.
- Turn off incoming voice and video calls so no outside callers or devices can attempt to access your speaker and lurk in your home, or worse yet, become privy to your private life.
- Remove sensitive or private data from any accounts to which you'll be linking via your smart speaker.
- Finally, as with any smart or Wi-Fi powered device, turn off the power on your smart speaker when you're not using it.

Turn Off Device Cameras and Microphones When Not in Use

Eavesdroppers can have a wide array of intentions: some lurk, some prank, while others watch your family and your home with more dastardly plans. The pranksters may make themselves known just to mess with you, but the more dangerous kind will remain silent.

To protect yourself from eavesdroppers, turn off your microphones and cameras when not in use. Sophisticated hackers can remote-start your computer or devices if they breach your network. A nontechnical step you can take to really dial up your security is to place a piece of dark tape over the camera. Duct tape for the win, again!

Make Sure Your Smart Home Security System Is Secure

Home security systems have gotten smart, and you can now gain peace of mind while away from your home by monitoring your home security system to rest assured that the system can alert local police if it's compromised. However, as with any smart device, you need to make sure that you're smart about your privacy and take the necessary steps to secure your smart security system. Here's a roundup of the best ways you can ensure that your smart home security system is, indeed, secure.

- Buy your smart security system from a trusted, reputable brand. Do your research!
- Make sure that you always run the recommended system updates. These updates contain the most advanced version of security protection available from the company.
- Disable any features of the smart home security system that you won't be using for your home.
- Change any default passwords or codes in the system when you set it up (and update them regularly).
- Consider setting up a separate Wi-Fi network in your home solely for the home security system. This way, if any device on your home network is hacked, giving a devious stranger access to your Wi-Fi, he won't have access to the home security system.

Turn Off Your Baby Monitors When You're Not Using Them

It takes a putrid kind of evil to hack a baby monitor and spy on precious infants or whole families, but there are individuals out there who've done it. It's wise to protect your baby and your family by being smart about how you use baby monitors in your home (particularly the smart versions that can connect to apps or your home Wi-Fi network).

Follow these tips:

- Use an old-school baby monitor where the most risk you'll have is some scrambled radio waves from time to time.
- If you want or need a video monitor to help keep your child healthy and safe, make sure you always turn off the monitor when you're not using it.
- Run software updates frequently. These updates include fixes and added security measures that are ever-evolving as criminals, voyeurs, or pranksters find more ways to access baby monitors.

Disconnect Your Baby Monitors from Wi-Fi

The smartest course of action is to not connect video monitors to your home Internet network. When you do, you're making it that much easier for a hacker to access a video feed of your sleeping baby or listen in on the private moments you share as a family. If someone is able to gain access to your network, she can usually get into any devices that are connected to it as well. That likely means she can see most, if not all, of the private information she'd need to steal your identity or run up credit card charges in your name.

If you must include a smart baby monitor in your child's nursery, make sure that you always disconnect it from Wi-Fi when you're not using features that need Internet access, and make sure to password protect the camera in your settings. This gives a hacker one more, much more difficult hoop to jump through. And the more hoops you can set up, the more secure and safe your home and family will be.

Secure Your Wearable Fitness Tracker Data

As great as wearable fitness devices are for your physical health, they present a risk to your privacy health. Like other Wi-Fi devices and apps, fitness trackers are prone to hacking, and they contain very sensitive data about your health that you probably wouldn't want to get into the wrong hands.

You can take some steps for privacy though:

- Make sure that you change your password frequently.
- Always run any updates needed on your device.
- Monitor your "access information" in your fitness tracker account access settings.
- Take the time to block unknown access requests. Look for names you don't recognize or log in details from locations you are not familiar with, and revoke them immediately.

Turn Off One-Click Ordering with Online Retailers

While one-click ordering can save you time when you're stocking up on home supplies or shopping for your family Christmas, it can also lead to accidental or fraudulent purchases. If your account is ever hacked, it will be even easier and faster for the perpetrator to place one order after another... *Click. Click. Click.*

You can easily minimize your risk by:

- Turning off one-click ordering in your online retail accounts.
- Removing your saved payment information. The extra couple of minutes it takes to enter your details for each order is time well spent to protect your private information and avoid fraudulent charges, should your account ever be hacked.

Beware of Stranger Danger

Background chatter is part of being in a crowded or busy location, but you've probably experienced a time when you could overhear someone talking about very private things in public—their relationship, finances, health, and so forth. You may even talk about such things when you're catching up with a friend or having a meal out with your significant other. There's no reason you cannot have a nice conversation in public, but sharing personal details loudly in public can violate your own privacy, or that of others if they're included in what you're saying. When you're out in public, particularly in crowded places, remember that others can hear you. There could be people who are listening whom you wouldn't want to know the private details of your life. So, keep it light in public conversations and save private discussions for somewhere, well, private. You never know who might be listening!

Embrace the Chip Reader
for Debit Payments

You may not think twice about the times each day that you enter your debit card PIN into a PIN pad to pay for gas, groceries, and many other purchases. The problem is that you're probably never (or rarely) the only person in line, and it is quite easy for the stranger in line behind you to peer over your shoulder. He can catch a glance of your debit card and watch you as you enter the PIN. Even the PIN pads that have the shields on the side don't require more than an extra crane of the neck if someone really wanted to peer in on you as you enter your PIN. In fact, stolen PINs at ATMs and PIN pads have become such a prevalent security and privacy issue that credit and debit card companies came up with a more secure solution that does not require a PIN but that validates your card through a chip embedded in it. At the moment, using the chip reader is the best option when it comes to using PIN pads. Wayward over-the-shoulder-peekers have nothing to look at and your transaction is approved safely in seconds.

No Chip Reader?
Sign That Dotted Line Then!

If you're making a purchase from a store that does not yet offer a chip reader, you can still protect your PIN from any suspicious onlookers by running your debit card as a credit card instead. This option should be available to you on the PIN pad, but if for some reason it isn't, ask the cashier to run your debit card as a credit transaction, and then sign for the transaction rather than entering your PIN. This easy step eliminates the risk that someone will see your PIN over your shoulder, and it doesn't take much more effort than punching in a PIN.

Don't Forget to Sign Out (Especially on Public Computers or Wi-Fi)

You probably have a computer that you use at work or, if you're a student, you may use public machines at the library or school. When you're on public machines, you should try to avoid accessing extremely sensitive accounts (such as your bank or credit card accounts), but if you are hankering for a quick scroll through social media or want to check your personal email, then you should still proceed with caution. Make sure you *always* log out of any of your accounts when you're on a public computer (for good measure and to build it into a habit, do it at home and on your mobile as well). If you don't log out of your accounts (even if you close the browser) the person who uses that computer after you could access those accounts when she opens up the same browser that you used. Logging out takes a split-second, but it's one of the best (and easiest) ways to protect your privacy on public computers or Wi-Fi networks.

Always Give the Printer or Copier a Final Glance

If you frequently need to make copies for your business or personal life, then it may be worth investing in a nice copier/scanner/printer that you can use at home, keep secure, and situate close to your personal shredder. However, if you're like a lot of people, you probably only need to make copies (particularly personal ones) on rare occasions. When your need to print arises and you head off to the library or local printing and shipping store to take care of your copying and scanning needs, make a conscious mental note to double check any machine you use and ensure you don't leave any documents behind. It is very easy to get distracted and leave something behind on the printer or inside the copy machine. Do not let that something be your personal information!

Be Picky about Where You Place Your Customer Loyalties

Punch cards, points toward prizes or discounts, and special pricing for members are some common loyalty tactics you're likely to see as you go about your daily business. Avoid the loyalty rewards that require you to provide your address, phone number, or any other information that's personal. You've likely seen the many news stories about big company data breaches, where a hacker has gained access to thousands—if not millions—of customer records. Customer loyalty details stored in a store's system are susceptible in such raids, so it's best to keep your information to yourself and stick to the simplicity and anonymity of the humble punch card.

Don't Share Your Birthday with Every Business or Restaurant in Town

As part of their customer loyalty or rewards programs, many stores and restaurants often ask for your birthday. It's seemingly harmless on the surface because they are usually offering to send you a free gift, a special coupon, or to give you a free dessert on your birthday. While their intentions are not malicious, it's prudent to keep your birthday out of superfluous databases and company records or systems. This information, coupled with past transaction records as a patron, can give a hacker much more ammo to compromise your identity should he breach the security of that system and gain access to that company's customer records. Never share your birthdate on forms or as part of a customer loyalty program in which the information will be stored.

Watch for Utility Bills or Charges You Don't Recognize

Setting up utilities (power, water, sewer, etc.) is a simple process. In fact, all you really need is a name and address to activate services at your home or apartment. Unfortunately, that information is very easy for others to get hold of and set up services in your name, for *their* home. This form of fraud is one you may never know about until you see charges or are denied an account with a utility service you've never used, due to large sums of past-due debt in your name. If you notice a bill for a utility service in a different name (but it comes to your house) or a charge comes through for a utility service you don't have, look into it. Alert that utility company you did not set up this account. Ask them to have their fraud department look into it for you.

Don't Share Streaming Video Account Passwords

You probably don't see the harm in letting your friend log in to your video streaming account to binge-watch that incredible new show everyone's talking about. But think about the data that's stored in your streaming account: your name, address, and billing details are all inside your account, and these types of accounts are all accessible by whoever logs in with your password. She can stream shows, sure, but she can also gain access to your settings and all the private details housed in that account. Never share your streaming video account passwords, even with trusted friends, because that text or IM you send could be intercepted and your password and private data could be exposed.

Use the Alerts Available on Credit Accounts

Your banking and credit accounts probably all offer an array of alerts that you can set up to monitor your balances and properly manage your finances. However, you can also use those alerts as booby traps for fraud by setting up notifications for large (or very small) purchases charged to your card. If you haven't been spending on a particular card, and an alert comes through that a charge has been made, you will know immediately that your card data is compromised. Or if you see that a couple of cents were charged to a card, you'll be able to take action before the larger fraudulent charge that is bound to be coming soon. Much of protecting your privacy is proactive, but setting these reactive trip wires to clue you in (where you may not otherwise notice suspicious charges) is also an important step in keeping your personal data safe.

Remove All Personal Information Before Selling, Donating, or Recycling an Old Computer

When the time comes for you to upgrade to a new computer or laptop, you should make sure that you completely remove all the personal information stored on your old machine before selling, donating, or recycling it. Take a careful inventory of everything on your computer, and make sure you remove all personal traces of you before placing it into anyone else's hands by following these guidelines:

- Delete all personal files
- Delete all your photos (after saving them on your new machine or external storage device)
- Uninstall all the programs you put on your machine
- Uninstall chat programs
- Uninstall the browsers you used on your machine
- Delete the hard drive to completely remove all traces of you from your computer

Change Your Passwords Any Time There's a Privacy Breach in the News

While it's somber, the fact is that there are always going to be data breaches. For every security measure that is in place, there's going to be a clever (but deviant) hacker who finds a way to infiltrate it. Whenever you see stories about data breaches in the news or hear about them from personal experiences of friends, you can take back some of your control by changing all your passwords. There may always be someone trying to get around protections, security, and passwords, but every time you change your password, you've made it that much harder for your privacy to be breached.

Never Write Down Your Passwords at Home or at Work

You probably have a lot of passwords to remember, and if you're doing your best to keep your privacy safe, you are also changing those passwords frequently. But resist the urge to write down your passwords. Scraps of paper and sticky notes are practically impossible to secure, and whether they're in your trash bin or on your desk, they're an unnecessary privacy risk. Keep your passwords in a secure password manager, and if you happen to forget one, reset it. You can never change your passwords too often.

CHAPTER 2

Protecting the Privacy of Your Children (and Teaching Them to Protect Themselves)

A s a parent, you're charged with overseeing the development of your children, and you work tirelessly to make sure that their lives are filled with all the love, support, and guidance they need, and more. You're the one who kisses their "owwies" better, cuddles them when they're sick, celebrates with them when they reach milestone after milestone, and guides their decision-making as they learn about the world around them and where they fit into it.

As a parent, you're not only responsible for keeping your own private details safe, you're also the one who's in charge of protecting your children's personal data (and teaching them how to keep themselves and their information safe). The moment your child is born, her paper trail of private information begins. She comes home from the hospital with a birthdate, medical records, a name, address, social security number, and birth certificate. This information is what scammers want to get their fingertips on.

These privacy protection hacks will help you understand just how to keep your children's private details safe as they grow and give you tips on how to build a strong foundation of privacy.

Don't Let Parental Controls Be Your Sole Privacy Solution for Your Kids

Parental controls can be a saving grace in a household where technology and children collide. Almost every device, program, or account you have should be equipped with parental control options so that you can manage what your children are able to watch on TV, look up online, or play on the computer or their favorite gaming system. These controls (which are typically found in the security settings) are necessary to protect your children online and preserve their innocence by keeping them from inadvertently accessing content that's inappropriate for them. You can also put measures in place to keep your children from purchasing on apps or online accounts by leveraging the power of parental control options. While you should embrace parental controls, don't rely on them as a "set and forget" approach to online security for your kids.

Teach Your Children What Privacy Truly Means (and Show Your Work with Examples)

Teach your children what privacy means and make sure they understand why rules are in place to protect them and your whole family. This will begin to create the framework they need to scrutinize the world around them and prepare for the day they will be responsible for protecting their own privacy.

When you start these conversations with your children though, privacy will just be a word. You need to add creative color and context around the term so that your children can create smart connections when they observe things happening around them and know how to react and behave. Examples are a great way to demonstrate how privacy works, and what information they can and cannot share at school or other public places when they're hanging out with friends.

Opt for Initials Only on Backpacks and Jackets

Naturally, you'll want to identify your child's items by doing things like writing his name inside the tag of his coat or adding a luggage tag to his backpack. This is something that you'll do with the very best intentions in mind and with hopes that you'll be able to recover your child's belongings that have been forgotten or left behind.

However, putting specific identifying information such as your child's name and address on clothes they wear or bags they carry can create unnecessary privacy risks for your child and your family. Instead, follow these guidelines:

- Don't use address tags on your child's school bag or even write or embroider his name on clothing and jackets.
- Do write his initials on jacket tags or iron on a fun patch with his initials. That will help you and your child identify their items among the sea of others in the lost and found at his school. This way, if someone who should not have these items does get them, she won't have any specific details that can pinpoint your child or your home.

Empower Children with the Privacy Protection Power of "No"

Teach your children that it's okay to say "no" when anyone at school (an older student, a teacher, the janitor, the lunch lady, etc.) asks them to share details about their lives that are private. Let them know that they do not have to defer to adults if those people are trying to violate their privacy by asking intimate details about:

- Your family life
- Where you live
- Where you work
- How much money you make
- Where you're going on vacation (and when)

Prepare your child with examples of information that is private and should not be shared and also let them know if he ever feels pressured or uncomfortable he should say "no," walk away, and tell you immediately.

Be the Wi-Fi Gatekeeper of Your Household

Giving your child unfettered access to the Internet will increase the likelihood she'll stumble into places she shouldn't be. She may fill out forms for a free giveaway or expose other private details without knowing better. Or she may start chatting with a "friend" online who seems trustworthy but is really trying to glean personal details for devious reasons.

You need to be the Wi-Fi gatekeeper of your household by following these tips:

- Keep your Wi-Fi password a secret, and only give it to your children during times that you've designated for them to be online.
- Put locked PINs on all your devices so that you have to unlock them in order to connect to the Internet.

Create a Code Word or Gesture for Privacy

You should create a code word or gesture that only your family members know, one that means "Don't ask that" or "Don't tell—that's private information." This way, if you're in public or see your child posting something online that is private to your family or borders on oversharing (private details about where you live, where you work, when you're leaving for vacations, etc.), you can enact the code word or gesture. If you go with a word, make it something obscure and random. Each time you're heading out into a public place, remind your children of the code word and what it means. If you have to use it, discuss it afterward.

If There's an App for That...There Should Be a Parent for It

App creators can be good people or bad people, and the apps created by the latter are usually a ruse or a hiding place for privacy-breaching crooks. Apps can also be a subtle way to access the surplus of personal data that lives on your smart devices. Pay attention when your children are downloading apps, and ensure that the apps aren't requesting access to personal details or programs on your phone that don't make sense. Why exactly would a crossword puzzle game need access to your device's camera or your contacts, for example? Thinking logically like this will help you weed out the bad apps much more quickly. Teach your children to think with the same reasoning and logic, and as they're learning what to look for, make a rule that they can only use apps you deem safe.

Other Online Risks
Kids Should Know

Sadly, there are bad people who use otherwise good apps as a vehicle for their evil plots. You've probably heard the harrowing news stories about apps that, on the surface, seem like innocent fun as games and photo sharing platforms. But that's just the mask the stranger who is using apps to gather personal details from children and teens wears. These kids may be more trusting and less savvy to the danger that can be built into apps. The apps will look and operate just like any others, but be on the lookout for apps that have a chat component. If your children have smartphones or tablets of their own, you should carefully monitor the apps that they're downloading and the programs they're using online. Always disable the chat setting if it's available on the app.

Oversee Any Surveys, Forms, or Giveaways

"Free Tablet Giveaway!"
"Earn Money Taking Surveys!"
"You've Been Selected for a $100 Gift Card!"

As your children are perusing online, it's very possible they'll happen upon surveys, giveaways, or other types of forms that promise to give them something amazing for free—well, for free as long as they fill out that form with private details such as their address, phone number, age, gender, etc. Some might even go so far as to ask for credit card information or ask personal questions that are an attempt to hack passwords. In a few seconds, a form can seriously jeopardize your privacy, and your children may not yet understand the risks when blinded by the prospect of a free gift.

Teach your children about the dangers of filling out forms asking for private information, and make sure they know to ask permission before filling out surveys or trying to get free things.

Disable Location Settings and Discourage Social Media Check-Ins

Most newer smart devices have GPS location capabilities built into them, which can be extremely convenient if you're traveling or going to a place you've never been before. Privacy issues are inherent in this feature though, because your child's smartphone can act as a beacon to his location. While this also has its benefits (if it's you trying to locate your child), displaying your location throughout the day raises serious privacy issues.

Help your children learn to protect their privacy by turning off location settings on their smart devices when they're not being used for a safety purpose. For older children who are savvy enough to turn location back on themselves, discourage them from checking into locations or posting with their location on while they're out with friends. Explain the risks so they know you're protecting them and not trying to steal their fun.

Be Smart about Luggage Tags (and Teach Kids to Plan Ahead)

Some of the very best memories you'll make with your children are during vacations and trips to visit family. If you're like most people, you probably didn't consider that a visible luggage tag could be a risk to your privacy. As you're planning your next family adventure, make sure that you have your luggage properly prepared with an address tag that slips discreetly into the luggage. This will help ensure that your home address isn't displayed openly on the exterior of your bag, where any peering eyes can see. You may want to use that alternate P.O. Box or street address you've set up to protect your home address.

Be a Privacy Advocate at Your Child's School

When you enroll your child in school, you are asked to provide a lot of sensitive data such as her birthdate, vaccination records, previous school records, and of course, all of your home address and contact information. While you need to give this type of information to your child's school, you are absolutely within your rights (and best judgment) to visit the school office and learn how they store records and make sure your child and family's data isn't accessible to others. Look for an assurance that the personal details you've provided to them are being kept safe and are not accessible to anyone other than the very small group of personnel at the school who need access. The school should not be too detailed or forthcoming (that's a red flag all its own) but they should be able to give you a rundown on how paper files are locked or convey that computer-managed systems are encrypted and secured to protect all the data from privacy breaches.

Oversee All Online Shopping in Your Household

Until your children mature and begin having money of their own, you'll need to guide their path in online shopping to teach them how to safely make purchases online (and protect your own finances at the same time). Oversee the online shopping in your home by:

- Teaching children how to look for safe and secure order forms.
- Showing children how to look for the markers of a safe shopping site, such as a web address beginning with "https" rather than "http." Many sites may also have secure purchasing seals, which can be easily faked. Always click through them and ensure they lead to a reputable site with a validation certificate for that seal.
- Deleting any saved payment details you have in online retail accounts.
- Never using auto-fill for account passwords or payment information.
- Mandating that your children only shop online with you or another parent present or with your permission.

Uphold an Open Dialogue Policy in Your Home Surrounding Privacy Concerns

An important part of protecting your privacy is encouraging an open dialogue at home and making sure that your children know they can (and should) tell you if they're ever being pressured for personal information. That's true whether the pressure is from anyone at school, on the bus, at the park, or any other place their day may unfold without your supervision. Make sure that your children know that nothing is too small to share with you. If it is something that tickled their intuition or made them feel uncomfortable, they need to know that they can tell you about it. If your child feels comfortable telling you about anything that gives him pause, then you can help continue shaping his intuition and decision-making skills (especially concerning privacy) even if you're not able to be with him every moment as he grows.

Teach Your Children Not to Share Your Home Wi-Fi Password

Once your children are old enough to know your Wi-Fi password, it's time to start teaching them how to protect their privacy and your family's privacy by safely using the Wi-Fi. One of the key lessons you need to include is when it's appropriate to share the Wi-Fi password (and more importantly, when it's not).

Teach children that they should not share your Wi-Fi password with friends unless it's authorized and overseen by you. Even if you know their friends well, you may not know exactly what privacy protections they have in place on their own devices. Connecting these devices to your home Wi-Fi network can expose your whole network to risk if they aren't practicing good security. If you trust the child, then connect her device for her and let her know the rules that your own children must follow when they're spending time online. When she's finished and heading home, disconnect her phone from your Wi-Fi and then change the password to keep your network safe and secure.

Never Disclose Your Spare Key Location or Share Your Home Security Code

Children are generally more trusting than world-weary adults, so they may not yet have that trip wire in their decision-making skillset that says, "Uh oh, that's not a good idea. Don't do or say that!" As they're developing their privacy protection prowess, you'll need to help guide their decisions surrounding your family's privacy, no matter how obvious the risk may seem to you. When it comes to showing your children how to protect home privacy, you can:

- Make a pact with your children to never share information about where you hide your spare key.
- Make sure your children know to *never* give out the code to your home alarm system, even to a friend.
- Teach children to only retrieve your spare key from its hiding spot when no one is looking.
- Teach children never to enter the home security code with a friend looking over their shoulder.

Help Your Children Set Up Their Privacy Settings on Social Media Accounts

As a parent, you're ultimately in charge of deciding when it's appropriate for your child to interact via social networks, but even when you deem him ready, it's vital that you oversee the setup of his privacy settings using guidelines such as these:

- Go into the settings of his social media account and navigate to the privacy and security options to customize and control his social interactions as much as possible on the platform.
- Hide personal information such as birthdate, city, relationship status, and location to keep private details blocked.
- Enhance your child's privacy protection further by putting controls in place for who can see his posts and pictures and who can put information on his wall, feeds, and timelines.
- Check back frequently to see if changes have been made to the security and privacy settings (because this happens all the time) and make sure you have all your child's private information secured or blocked from being seen by the social masses online.

Teach Your Children about Private Posts and Pictures

It's quite easy to set up privacy settings in online accounts and social media platforms—so easy a child could probably do it. Your child. This is why it's not only important to check often that your child's online privacy is intact, but also to begin teaching her about the importance of privacy settings by:

- Making sure your children understand the difference between public and private posts. (Once they move a post or photo to public, it's fair game for all the antsy fingers on the Internet).
- Teaching children how to discern what information is okay to share with a select group of friends and what kinds of information should never be shared online.
- Never assuming anything is obvious to your children when it comes to privacy protection, because it may not be.

Teach Children to Say Something If They See Something

If someone your child is friends with suddenly begins posting weird things on your child's social media page or starts sending him malicious messages out of the blue (and not provoked by anything in real life) then your child may not know how to react. If there's no reason at all behind these types of posts or messages, there's an extremely high likelihood that his friend's social media account has been hacked. But your child's mind probably won't go there first. He'll probably be hurt, confused, or offended and may be tempted to ask what's going on or engage with that person in some way, which could put his privacy at risk. This is exactly how hackers gain access to other accounts, by being salacious to get a response.

You should teach your child that hackers hide behind this kind of behavior, and if he sees it, he should:

- Step away from the computer, tablet, or phone and tell you about the odd behavior he's seeing.
- Contact his friend (outside of social media) who supposedly sent the unprovoked and malicious message and let that person know about the messages or posts so he can change his password and adjust his privacy settings to get the hacker out of his account pronto.

Caution Kids about the Friends-of-Friends Loophole

You need to advise your children and teens about the "friends-of-friends" loophole as they're interacting with friends on social media. Show them how to adjust their privacy settings to make sure that friends of friends cannot see their posts or profiles. In this one single degree of separation, a post with too much private information could easily be seen by a friend of a friend, and that person may not actually be your friend's friend. They could be a stranger or someone who slipped under their radar as a hacker. If your child's friend doesn't have his privacy settings updated for optimal protection, it's very easy for one post to get onto the screens of many strangers. Make sure your child turns off the friends-of-friends setting in her social media account, so she keeps her social circle to only people she knows.

Teach Children to Be on the Lookout for Copycat "Friends"

One somewhat amateur (but still quite effective) tactic floating about on social media platforms is copycats. They're not quite hackers, but they're clever and use work-around channels to try and get a peek at private data.

If photos aren't private, a copycat can save a photo without ever being in the actual account, sign up for a new account with that picture, and start trying to add friends to the "new" account—all while posing as someone he isn't. This tactic is effective because kids may turn off their profiles or delete them and then change their mind and make a new one. Their friends may not really be concerned if they see a friend request from someone they already think they're friends with online, especially if the new fake profile has that friend's picture. Teach your children to be on the lookout for fake friends and copycats on social media by:

- Checking their list of friends to see if their "friend" trying to add them is missing.
- Contacting that friend (outside of social media) to let them know they have a copycat so the friend can report the profile and get it shut down.

Teach Children to Never Share Photos of Strangers Online

As your children learn more from you about how privacy protection works and why it's important, they probably assume that the tips and advice you're passing on to them should flow outward to others as well. But they are still just kids and will be prone to making decisions without a lot of forethought. They may follow the crowd out of a desire for acceptance even if they have a nagging feeling inside that something isn't quite right.

For example, if they see someone doing a cool skateboard move and take a video, that's not necessarily a privacy violation, but if they happen upon someone who's crying in public and talking about private matters such as losing his job, financial troubles, medical issues, etc., then taking a video and posting it on social media is very much a privacy concern. Teach your child to always respect the privacy of others and never exploit it for a like or a share online. It's just good privacy karma.

Teach Children to Never Share Their Phone PIN

It's important to teach your children early that they should never share the PIN to their phone, even with their friends. Mobile phones connect to Wi-Fi and also contain a large amount of personal data in apps, email accounts, banking information, etc., so while they're handy and fun, they're also a common target for privacy invasions. Children typically don't think like this though. They recognize their phone as a source of fun and will probably want friends or classmates to share in that fun. But all it takes is the wrong person accessing your child's phone to put your privacy at risk through a click on a malicious ad or a visit to a site riddled with malware. Make sure that your children understand that their phone PIN is just as important as a password used to secure their online accounts. You can refer to their phone PIN as a unique password to help them make the connection between PINs and privacy.

Carefully Monitor
Online Gaming

Online gaming is extremely popular among teens, and while it's fun for your kids to play online with friends in teams to accomplish missions, you should pay attention to what games your children are playing. This is particularly true if the games operate through your Wi-Fi. Monitoring gaming with an eye open for privacy concerns involves:

- Steering clear of the popular free game of the moment (hackers and data lurkers salivate over these because free games aren't as heavily secured, and anyone can join and play—including the ill-intentioned).
- Watching your child play her game for a while, and keeping an eye out for ads that may pop-up.
- Setting up a separate Wi-Fi connection solely for gaming so no one can lurk onto your home Wi-F and into the private data you have in other connected devices.
- Removing all personal information and banking details from the game settings.

Don't Allow Your Children to Game with Strangers

While gaming attracts teens with a nearly magnetic force, it also tends to attract fraudsters and hackers. Many of the online games available today allow you to connect with friends and play and interact with others who enjoy the game. However, this is where ill intentions are easily disguised as a fellow gamer, and your children will be tempted to interact and play with people they do not know. This is a huge privacy risk because these smooth operators take advantage of their gaming connection and earn trust by playing alongside your child in a game. This can quickly turn into ploys for personal information that your child may not catch as dangerous because she sees this person as a kindred spirit. Only allow your children to connect with friends you know and trust, and keep your privacy protected by restricting your child's gaming circle to real-life friends.

Disable Chat in Online Games

The chat feature in online games is probably the single biggest risk to your family's privacy. This is where strangers can reach out to your children as fellow gamers and gain their trust by giving them tips and playing games along with them in a team setting. It's happened time and again: a rogue gamer gains the trust of a child and asks for his password to upgrade his character or give him special pieces needed in the game. The gamer then infiltrates the whole family's privacy by hacking the Wi-Fi and gains access to loads of personal data. While you should teach your children about the dangers lurking in online gaming chats, you should also disable the feature in the settings of the game to remove the temptation and keep your privacy safe.

Centralize the Location of Your Family Computer

There are undoubtedly a lot of privacy risks inherent in allowing your children to spend time online or on their devices. If your child has a laptop, phone, or computer in her room behind a closed door, she's much less likely to think about all your warnings or practice good discretion online. As you're teaching your children how to keep their privacy (and yours) safe, it's a good idea to centralize the family computer in a main room in the home where you can keep an eye on what exactly your child's doing online. If your children have their own laptops, tablets, or phones, you can make a policy as to where they can use them online—in a shared living space with you present.

Teach Your Children Everything New You Learn about Privacy Protection

Protecting your privacy and teaching your children how to keep their own information safe offline and online, is an ever-evolving process. Every time you learn a new tip or strategy to keep your personal data better guarded, tell your kids about it too. Make this communication two-way by asking your children what they know about privacy protection. They may have tips you don't know about. They'll probably surprise you with how savvy they are.

CHAPTER **3**

Strategies for Protecting Yourself and Your Private Data on Mobile Devices

Depending on your age, you may remember a time when the whole family shared one telephone, and it was connected to the wall in a central part of your home such as the kitchen or living room. If you had siblings you had to stake your claim on the phone to call your friends, and you likely had to suffer the embarrassment of your parents picking up the line and overhearing you gush about your current crush.

One of the most remarkable communication innovations of the past twenty years was the birth of the mobile phone. Almost every person goes about his or her day with a tiny computer, camera, phone, and connection device that fits in his pocket. It's amazing really, but that tiny mobile device—one that you could not imagine life without—houses masses of personal information about you and your life. Your phone contains your contacts, address, and photos—and can connect to your email, social media, and the Internet with a simple tap. More than any other device you own, it opens you up to privacy risks. This is partly because you're on such familiar terms with it that you may not be as careful on your mobile as you are on your computer. I mean, it's a phone…right?

This collection of mobile privacy protection hacks will help you enjoy the freedom in life that mobility offers, while also protecting your privacy details.

Secure All of Your Devices with Strong Passwords or PINs

It seems obvious that you should protect your portable devices like your phone, tablet, and laptop with strong passwords or PINs because they go with you to various locations in some configuration almost every day.

But having to enter a password or PIN *every* time you access one of your devices is kind of inconvenient, so if you're like a lot of people, you may opt for not using these protections. After all, you always have your devices in your care, right? Right. Until you don't. Your devices all house an abundance of personal information that would be devastating to your life if it got into the wrong hands. Unfortunately, it's easy to leave a device behind, have it fall out of your bag, or stolen from you.

Lock every device you regularly take with you. Make your passwords and PINs random and creative, and use different ones on all your devices.

Check the Permissions on Preloaded Apps

Whenever you upgrade your phone, you probably notice all the apps that come preloaded onto your new device. Or maybe you don't. If you do, you probably get so used to seeing them on your screen that you don't really think about them much. That can be problematic for your privacy though, because those preloaded apps may have default settings that give the app permission to your phone data, camera, or microphone. Any time you get a new phone, take a couple of minutes to put your privacy protection in check by doing the following things:

- Look through all the preloaded apps on your phone and delete or uninstall the ones you'll never use.
- Go into the settings on your phone and find where the permissions on each app are located.
- Go into each app and turn off access to personal data, location, camera, and phone.
- Check app permissions after each app or phone update to make sure your permissions are set to your liking.

Watch for Unexplained Diminished Battery Life

If you're playing games, accessing Wi-Fi, or streaming videos on your mobile device, you already know those activities can drain your battery much faster than other things you do with your phone. But if you notice that your battery seems to drain more quickly than it should, and you're constantly having to charge it despite not using apps that require a lot of battery life, this could be a symptom of a hack. If a con artist has gained access to your phone, then he could be passing data through apps or even through the text messaging feature on your phone. If your battery drains for no reason, you can investigate further using these steps:

- Check all the permissions on every app on your phone. If you notice any have been changed to allow access to your phone, camera, location, or microphone, uninstall the app immediately.
- Look through your text messages and see if you notice anything suspicious (most hackers clean up after themselves but it's worth checking).
- If you still have an issue, you may have to restore your phone to factory settings, after backing up all your data and photos.

Don't Allow Any Notifications on Your Lock Screen

If you've disabled the push notifications from your phone apps, then you are taking a step in the right direction for privacy protection. But you need to go a step further when it comes to notifications. When you were disabling your app push notifications, you probably didn't think about the messages that you have set up to pop-up on your phone when you get a new email or text, or when your bank sends you your daily balance via text. Think about them now. Those types of notifications are all typically set up to appear on your lock screen so they get your attention and you know to open them. But if someone were to get hold of your phone (even if they can't get around your PIN), they could still learn personal details about you by the lock screen notifications. You can disable these in your phone settings, and you should in the name of your privacy.

Pay Attention to Sudden Surges in Your Data Usage or Phone Bill

Sudden spikes in your data or unexpected charges on your phone bill can be indicators that fraudulent activity is happening on your phone. If you notice that your data usage is way up or your bill surges unexpectedly, and there's no explanation for it or any changes in how you use your data, then it could mean a hacker has accessed your phone and could be using your data maliciously. If this happens, contact your mobile provider and have them walk through the charges. They can also help you pinpoint times of day the spikes are happening, so you know what to watch for. For good measure change all your passwords, and check the permissions on your apps to block the hack from continuing.

Avoid Using Data or Wi-Fi at a Crowded Event, Festival, or Demonstration

Whenever you're at an event in a public place, you should limit how you use your phone data and be cautious of Wi-Fi networks set up for the particular festival, concert, or event that you're attending. Scammers and hackers follow large events, and if they notice there's an open Wi-Fi network provided, then they'll probably be lurking on it to see what kinds of personal information they can access. When you use the Wi-Fi to upload pictures, post on social media about the event, or send texts to your friends, the hackers will move in. Staying off your phone as much as possible during big events can help you stay out of the hacker's grasp and reduce the risk your personal data will be compromised or your messages intercepted.

Take Advantage of Content Filters

You may have noticed that your mobile carrier is putting information on its website or on your account login page regarding content filters that are now available. Content filters are somewhat like parental controls but on steroids. They're a level of protection you can use to protect every mobile user in your family by setting up preferences about what kinds of content you want to be able to access from your phone, whether on Wi-Fi or 4G. You can set up content filters to block your children from inappropriate content or sites you don't want them visiting, and you can also control what types of ads or marketing you want to be shown on your phone.

Hint, big time hint, nay overt recommendation: choose no ads whatsoever. Ads can be a gateway to scams and trouble when it comes to privacy, so it's best to keep them off your phone altogether to avoid a bad ad that slips through the cracks with the intent to jeopardize your identity or personal information on your phone.

Auto-Lock Your Screens

While you were checking your phone and responding to your texts, did you leave your work up on your laptop screen? When you went back to your laptop, did you leave your phone next to you, but with the screen still open to your text messages? Did anyone walk by your table or scoot around the back of your chair while you toggled devices?

These are the kinds of things you should think about when you're using technology in public. It only takes mere seconds for someone to walk by and peep in on the private details you view on your various screens, and there's more time for lurkers to look in on your screens if you're moving between them and not locking or closing one while you use another. It's a great idea to stay mindful of what's on your screens and who may be privy to it. You can also do yourself a huge favor by setting up your device screens to go dark and lock after a couple seconds of inactivity. You can manage this from the settings, and set it up so that your screen will turn off and your phone will lock after as little as five or ten seconds of inactivity. Don't give those prying eyes enough time to see anything private on your devices!

Get Off the Phone Grid with Alternate Phone Numbers

Despite your best efforts to keep your mobile phone number private by not filling out forms or not providing your phone number in unnecessary situations, it's quite possible that you'll still end up on a local telemarketing list. This can be intrusive and open you up to a barrage of calls from people who are trying to sell you something or get a donation for the charity of the moment. Additionally, there may be times when you need to add your phone number for account validation or contact purposes in your online accounts. If these places where your phone number lives are ever breached or if your information gets sold to a telemarketing list (whether inadvertently or intentionally) then we still arrive back at the same truth: your phone number is out there, and it opens you up to risk when it comes to your privacy.

However, there is a solution that can get you a bit further from the main bustle of the cell phone grid and keep your mobile number as exclusive and private as possible. That option is to set up an alternate phone number through a free or low-cost voice program. You can use this alternate phone number to fill in forms or associate to your accounts and keep your personal number much more personal. Make sure you choose an established, reputable company and never make any personal calls on your alternate number.

Forward Your Alternate Phone Number to Your Personal Mobile Phone Number

Once you've set up your alternate phone number through a trusted voice solutions company, you can take one more easy step to simplify your phone life and ensure that you're maintaining the privacy of your personal number: embrace call forwarding. Within your voice account, you can set up call forwarding so that any calls that come through to your alternate phone number will be passed along to your personal mobile number, and the caller will be none the wiser. This is a feature you can turn on and off as you please. To avoid those dreaded telemarketing calls or spam-ridden recordings that can call you, you should leave this feature off for the most part.

Understand the Risks of Biometric Device Protection

In recent years, mobile providers have been making strides to enhance device protection with biometric options (like fingerprints) for unlocking a device. Your fingerprint is unique to you. It seems like a perfect option for protecting your devices and all the personal data you keep stored on your phone. However, before you set up biometric validation on your smart devices, you should consider the risks inherent to this process. In order for your phone to validate you by your fingerprint, it must store your fingerprint to make the match each time you open up your phone. If someone were to gain access to your phone and get hold of your fingerprint, this could have devastating results on your life and any extremely sensitive information your fingerprint protects. For example, an advanced (and especially sinister) crook could quietly steal your phone from your bag in a public café and then lift your fingerprint off your drinking glass with a modest dab of glue. Once dry, this glue fingerprint could be used to bypass the security measure on your smartphone. Sound inconceivable? Google it, and you'll find an array of tutorials showing just how easy it is to mimic a fingerprint and trick a "smart" device. This is a trend worth watching, though, and you should keep your finger on the pulse of how it's developing; just be careful about protecting that finger's print in the meanwhile.

Don't Unlock Your Phone
with Your Face

Some of the new mobile devices also offer an option to unlock your device using facial recognition software. While this seems like a step up in mobile security measures, it's actually one of the less secure options you can use to keep all the private information on your phone protected. Think about all the photos of your face that are online: in your social media accounts, in databases, etc. The fact is, it's probably not very hard to find a photo of you online if someone really wants it, and if he also happens to get his hands on your phone he can trick the facial recognition software quite easily with a mere photo and access all the personal details you keep stored in your phone.

Disable Bluetooth
When You're Not Using It

While Bluetooth technology is convenient (and really quite cool since to the naked eye it looks a little like magic) it can also be a huge privacy concern. When you connect Bluetooth-enabled devices, they merely have to both be powered on and have the Bluetooth enabled to connect and share data. You should always turn off Bluetooth on your phone when you're not using it. If your Bluetooth is always on, you're offering an open-door policy to Bluetooth-savvy crooks. You'd never intentionally sign such a deal, but you don't have to. Hackers can gain access to your phone easily if you leave your Bluetooth on all the time, and it can happen without you even knowing what has occurred.

Research Apps Before You Install Them on Your Mobile Devices

There is an app for almost anything you can think of, from gaming and entertainment to business and finance, to connection and collaboration and every nook and cranny in-between. Apps also have a dark side: they can often be a front for much more devious intentions than playing a fun game. Additionally, apps that aren't developed well or have weaknesses or glitches in the coding, are more susceptible to being hacked, which can put your personal privacy at risk if you have that app on your phone. You can choose apps more carefully by paying attention and following these rules:

- Be mindful of the apps you're loading onto your phone.
- Read through user reviews in the app store and do your own research online about any issues associated to the app or glitches people frequently experience.
- Pay attention and stay away from any apps that sound glitchy (meaning they crash and reload and never quite perform the function they set forth to do). Glitches are both a gateway and a symptom of fraudulent hacks.
- Do your research and use your best judgment before ever installing an app to your phone.

Pay Attention to What Apps Ask to Access

Once you've done your due diligence on researching an app you're interested in having on your smartphone, it's time to download it and install it on your phone. But pay attention to the details that are displayed when you get to this step. There will usually be a line of text that indicates what the app needs access to in order to function, and it will notify you if the app contains ads or in-app purchases. Pay attention to this information with a discerning eye because you can spot sketchy apps before they get onto your phone. A general rule for safely using apps is to avoid any that ask for access to your personal information, contacts, phone settings, other apps, or the camera. Now, there are exceptions. For example, if you're looking at an app for editing your photos, then it makes sense that it would need access to your photos (but not the camera itself). However, if you're loading a word search game and it wants access to your camera or personal data, be leery and don't download that app. If it seems especially weird or bordering on sketchy, you may want to report it to the app store for review.

Manually Adjust App Settings

As soon as you've finished installing an app, your fingers are probably just itching to start playing your new game or checking out all the cool features and gizmos it offers. But you need to take another important step first to further ensure that you are using your app safely and that the app does not present any hidden threats to your personal data and privacy. Many apps will load onto your phone with default settings, and some of those may leave you less than secure. Before you start using a new app:

- Go to your phone settings and find where all of your app preferences are located.
- From there, you can click into the settings for that app and turn off push notifications and app access to other parts of your phone like the camera or contacts. Then you can manage all your other privacy settings associated with the app.
- Always check your app settings any time you run an update to the app (as this will often restore those default settings) and check on all your app settings periodically to make sure nothing has changed in your privacy settings.

Remove App Access to Your Camera

You should be very cautious about any apps that ask for camera access, or any that you download and discover have camera access as a default permission. Always check new apps (and existing ones periodically) to make sure that your camera is not accessible to the app. If it is, if the app gets hacked (or has a devious app creator) it can mean that you've given someone access to watch you as you go about your day—and you probably take your phone everywhere. Check your settings often, and make sure no apps are accessing your camera without your knowledge.

Block Apps from Microphone Access

While you're checking your app permissions to disconnect apps from your camera, you should do a check for those that have microphone access at the same time. There are very few apps that should require access to your microphone, so if you see any that seem suspicious, uninstall those apps immediately. Someone could be listening to you throughout the day and overhearing all kinds of private details about you. For chat or video meeting apps you may be using, only enable the camera and microphone just before you use the app for a call and keep access forbidden any other time.

Password Protect Your Apps

While not all apps are equipped with a password option, many are, so you should use this extra layer of protection whenever possible, particularly with apps that access private accounts or contain personal information. You can see if apps offer password protection by going into the settings portion of your phone and navigating to your app permissions. When you click into an app's permissions settings, you'll see if a password or lock protection is offered. Use it if so, and remember to keep the password as strong, random, and unique as possible.

Make Sure Apps Don't Continue Running in the Background

When you exit an app, that doesn't always mean that you've shut down its function entirely. Many times, apps will continue to run in the background (which will be evident if notifications keep popping up on your phone even when you have the app closed). These apps can not only diminish your battery life but can also put your personal data at risk. Each time you finish using an app, don't just close it. Log out if possible (particularly on sensitive account apps) and make sure you've set up your app permissions to not allow apps to run in the background when they're not in use.

Avoid Clicking Any Link
Delivered via Text

As a general rule for keeping your phone (and all the personal data about you it contains) safe, you should never click on links or files that you're sent via text message. This is especially important if texts from unknown numbers come through because those are more obvious phishing scams. Phishing is a fraudulent tactic that scammers use to try and obtain your sensitive information, using messages or communications that catch your attention and seem (almost) believable. The key word is "almost" because a phishing scam (even a good one) will always give itself away if you know what to look for. Be on the lookout for messages containing links that come from people you do know. If you see a text with a link in it, check with the person who sent it to you (in another communication channel aside from text) and see if that person truly did send it to you and ask what it is. It's possible that person's phone has been hacked and the perp could be sending texts with links to pass along a virus to gain even more information from all her contacts.

Keep Messaging Apps
Off Your Mobile

In general, you should keep messaging apps off your mobile because they're particularly risky where your privacy is concerned. They often try to sync with your personal contacts, and they require access to the camera and microphone features of your device to facilitate your video chats or calls. These apps will also contain your location, personal information, and often ask you to store payment details so you can pay for calls or credits to make calls from the app to cell phone numbers. If anyone is able to access your phone or your messaging app, he'll have a wealth of personal information at his fingertips (and the information of all your contacts could be just a few clicks away).

Don't Sync Messaging Apps to Your Personal Contacts

While messaging apps are great for staying connected to all the important people in your life, there are some privacy concerns you should know about so you can enjoy your connections without exposing your personal information. Many of these apps will immediately ask to sync your contacts to make sure you have all your contacts on that app. When the app can access your contacts it'll sync them ,which basically means it saves a copy of all your personal contacts into its database. That seems far less convenient now, right? To keep your personal data (and the data of all your personal friends you have stored in your phone) safe, you should avoid syncing your personal contacts with any messaging apps that you use.

Enable Phone-Finding and Remote-Wipe Features or Apps on Your Phone

You should always pay attention and stay diligent in your efforts to keep your phone in your care, but in the event something happens and you are parted from it, it's good to have some safeguards in place. Have reputable phone-finding and remote-wiping apps on your phone. In the event your phone is lost or stolen, you can try to locate it via the phone finder, but even then it may be too late to preserve your privacy. There are also remote-wiping apps that you can use from another trusted device to clear all the data off your phone should it ever be stolen. Head off the crook by removing all that personal information before he has time to access it and use it against you. You will no longer have your data if you're forced to remote wipe your phone, but neither will a thief.

Restore Your Device to Factory Settings and Wipe Your Phone Before Selling, Upgrading, or Donating It

Technology moves with the speed of light, and you'll probably find yourself upgrading your devices, whether through the carrier, selling, or donating them. Make sure you take inventory of all the data that's on the device you'll be upgrading from. You can have the mobile tech at the store transfer your contacts and apps so that you're all set to go on your new phone, but if you're trading in your old device, make sure the manufacturer wipes it and restores it to factory settings. Request that the staff does it in front of you and make sure that everything personal to you is removed from that phone before it leaves your possession. You should do the same thing if you're going to donate or sell an old phone. You can carefully go through and delete all the photos, contacts, and apps and then restore the settings from the phone itself. Make sure you don't miss anything, because you don't know what hands that phone will pass through when it leaves you, and you don't want to hand personal details over to strangers to find in their "new to them" phone or tablet.

Don't Get Personal on Public Wi-Fi

While it is a great convenience and freedom to get online outside your home or office, you should be very careful about what you access on your phone while you're connected to public Wi-Fi. The downfall of public or open Wi-Fi in coffee shops, hotels, restaurants, etc. is that anyone can access them. That "anyone" may include hackers or other snoops who are trying to glean personal details from an open connection. You should avoid accessing any personal information such as your banking statements or accounts, medical records, and even your personal email or social networks while you're on public Wi-Fi. When you're connected, anything you do could be being watched by someone else.

Use Your Data to Connect While Traveling or in Public Places

If you're traveling or in public and need to access personal information using your phone, then you should use your phone's 4G data to browse and gather the information you need. This is not a fail-safe, and it doesn't necessarily mean that you should use your data to access private information with 100 percent confidence you're secure. But the 4G networks are held to a higher security standard so any browsing you do using your 4G connection will have more encryptions and protections in place to shield your information from wayward eyes. Make it quick, and only use this as an emergency backup plan when a secure connection isn't available to you.

Don't Answer or Respond
to the Unknown

If you've begun receiving calls from unknown numbers that call frequently and often around the same time each day, you may have a persistent telemarketer on your hands. You may also have gotten yourself on some kind of fraudulent calling scheme list. Maybe you entered your phone number on a form or an online retailer you shop with frequently (who has your phone number on file) has been breached. You can search the phone number online, see if other people are receiving calls, and determine if the number is part of a known fraud ring. Fraudsters don't just operate in phone calls and recordings; they can also send texts to your phone, which are even more problematic when it comes to protecting your privacy from a barrage of calls and texts you don't want to receive. Avoid answering calls from unknown or suspicious numbers, and if you receive odd texts, don't even open them. Worms and malware can be sent through text and will be activated if you open or respond to the message.

Permanently Block Calls or Texts from Suspicious Numbers

If you're getting calls or texts from unknown or questionable numbers and you've looked them up online to discover that other people are receiving malicious calls or texts too, you should immediately block those numbers. You can block the number directly from your phone by opening the call or text log and choosing the block number option. This will keep calls and texts from coming to your phone and help keep you and your data out of the hands of these fraudsters. You can also report the number to your mobile carrier as well to have it permanently blocked.

Stay Diligent During Mobile and Media Mergers

When companies merge, they sync their data and customer records into their new conglomerate. It's during these busy, yet quite sensitive, times that small windows or weak points in both company's databases may open. Advanced hackers are so subtle that you'll likely never notice they've been in your devices or information until it's too late. The ones who know how to look for company weak points know that companies are most susceptible to a breach during times of intense change and/or during massive data migrations. Here's how to stay diligent if your mobile provider is merging with another company:

- Stay alert, and keep a close eye on all your private details to make sure nothing strange is going on, like changes in your streaming or mobile accounts.
- If you do see anything, however small or slight, notify your carrier immediately.
- Keep your phone off Wi-Fi and turn it off whenever you're not using it to ensure that none of your private details are hacked.
- It may also be prudent to change your passwords on your mobile and streaming accounts more frequently during mergers. It's much harder to hack a moving target.

Delete Messages You Receive When Recovering or Resetting an Account Password

It's going to happen: with all the passwords you have in your life, you're going to forget one, and you'll need to reset it (by following the secure channels provided to validate your account and gain access to your personal information once more). If you're doing a password reset or recovery through a secure system, you'll be sent an email with a link or code, or maybe even a text message to validate that you are initiating the password request. Once you've changed your password, make sure that you delete all the emails and codes that you received during the process so that no one else can try and use them to change your password.

These codes and emails can also work as an alert system for you. If you receive a text or an email about an account password change request and you have *not* initiated it, you should immediately contact the support team or fraud department of that company or institution immediately.

Double Down with Two-Factor Authentication Whenever Possible

You may have noticed that your email provider and maybe other online accounts or programs offer an added layer of account control known as "two-factor authentication." When you enable this feature, in your email program, for instance, you're asked to enter your mobile phone number associated with your account. Then, whenever you log in to your email, you'll be taken to a screen that requires you to enter a code that you've been sent via text message to your mobile phone. When you enter the code, this serves as validation that you are the account owner and takes you into your inbox to navigate your email like normal. While you should ensure that the places you enable two-factor authentication are trusted and reputable, it's a good idea to enable this feature. This way, if anyone is trying to hack your email, you'll know immediately when you receive a code that you didn't initiate by logging into your account. This extra step can help you keep your email and other online accounts safer by requiring authentication from a trusted device. If you notify the platform immediately, you may have a hand in helping catch that scoundrel trying to breach your privacy and break into your email.

Delete Any Apps or Accounts
You No Longer Use

If you're not using an app anymore or have a collection of online accounts you never access, delete them. If an account is left unattended, it could be compromised, and you'd never know since you aren't in there often enough to notice changes or see red flags. Plus, it's never a good idea to leave your information sitting unattended in an account or app. You wouldn't leave your wallet, ID, and debit and credit cards unattended just because you didn't like the wallet anymore. All the data inside is still viable and important to you. The same is true for your forgotten accounts and apps. Ditch the wallet, but save your personal information.

Consider Paid Apps
over Free Ones

At first glance, it seems like the free app would be the best option. I mean it's free, and it is basically the same as the paid version, but with a couple ads here and there, right? Not quite. While you can access many of the same features in the free version of the app, you're not technically a customer of that app creator if you haven't paid for a service, so there isn't the same level of security on free apps as paid ones. When you pay for an app, you become a customer and you have more rights protected should anything happen to jeopardize your privacy while using the app.

Plus, those ads (on top of being annoying) are a breeding ground for fraud. They may lead you to an unsafe website looking to gather your information in exchange for some coins to use in the game, or they may be trying to get you to install another app that is intended for hacking or stealing private data. Paying for your apps helps eliminate many risks to your privacy, and isn't your privacy worth an investment of $2.99?

Take Social Media Apps Off Your Phone

Social media apps not only contain a wealth of private information, they also provide a gateway to all your friends' information as well. If your phone is ever stolen or a hacker is able to access your phone or the Wi-Fi network your phone is connected to, then he'll be able to easily access your social apps from your phone (which is one of the first places he's going to look for a big bulk data grab). But he can't look if those apps aren't on your phone.

Sync Your Smartphone with Your Smartwatch

Smart devices can be tethered together with Bluetooth technology, so if you have both a smartphone and a smartwatch, you should link them and activate the alerts smartwatches typically offer that let you know if your connected smartphone gets too far away from your watch. Your smartwatch will be on your wrist so it will be much harder for a stranger to discreetly sneak away with it in a public place. However, your phone may be sitting on a table or in a bag and will be more prone to thieving hands. If your phone is taken, your smartwatch will alert you when the phone gets just a few meters away from it. Often, this distance isn't enough to allow for the criminal to access anything on your phone before you're alerted and can take action to protect your data.

Never Charge Your Phone at a Public Charging Station

Even if your battery is blinking red, you should never charge your phone at a public charging station that offers its own USB charging cord. Most smartphones can be charged with a USB cord, but do you know what else USB cords can do? They can pass data between devices. If you plug into a public charging station or use one of the charging cords offered in a rideshare car, you're opening yourself up to the risk that the station or driver is trying to pull personal information off your phone with the USB cord. Always bring your own charging cord along with you, and only plug it into electrical outlets (not USB ports) when you're out in public.

CHAPTER 4

Strategies and Best Practices for Staying Safe and Protecting Your Privacy Online

A huge portion of your life probably exists or functions through online channels. You may do online banking or pay all your bills through online accounts rather than paper statements and handwritten checks. You may use social channels to connect with your family and friends. You probably use email, IMing, or texting as a main part of your work and personal communications.

The Internet has changed the fabric of our society in such a way that it's impossible to go back to outdated practices or ways of doing things. You probably wouldn't want to anyhow, due both to the convenience the Internet has brought to your life and the fact that online channels are updated with security measures more frequently than before. But the Internet is still a bit like the wild, wild west. There are new uses being discovered every day, both for good and for evil, so it's important you have a strong grasp on how to keep all your private details safe while you're surfing the web.

These privacy protection hacks include tips, strategies, and best practices that will help you enjoy the advantages of the Internet, while protecting your privacy.

Upgrade Your Router Regularly

You should upgrade your router every year or so to make sure that you are using current technology. If you are using significantly out-dated hardware, it will not be equipped with all the most modern protections needed to keep your Internet connection functioning fluidly and safely. If you're upgrading to a faster Internet connection speed that's now available in your area (finally!), always ask for a router upgrade as part of your new Internet package. It shouldn't cost any more than your standard router purchase or monthly rental fee, and it will ensure that you not only get to take full advantage of that fast connection but that there are all the updated protections in place to keep someone from pulling a fast one on your privacy.

Put Protections in Place to Block Malware and Viruses (and Run Updates Often)

Malware is malicious software that is designed to harm devices by disabling functions or creating system weaknesses as entry points for hacks. Malware can completely destroy one computer or even take down entire networks of devices and systems. You should never skip the step of adding antivirus and malware-blocking software to your computer. It's not an added gimmick based on fear or an unnecessary cost. It's a necessity to protect your computer (and all your personal information it contains) from hackers who use viruses or malware to infiltrate machines with the intent to steal your data or wreak havoc on your computer system. Antivirus software and malware blockers are designed to automatically protect your computer from known hacks, viruses, malware, ransomware, and worms that hackers may use to create a weakness in your computer system and gain entry.

This is why it's important to not only have these protection systems in place but to update them frequently to make sure you're protected from all the most current dangers lurking outside your computer as you navigate around the Internet. New hacks, viruses, and malware are created every day, so you increase your chances of protecting your computer with updated antivirus software.

Upgrade Your Passwords to Passphrases

There's a solution to simplify your password overload *and* increase the security of your passwords. Don't just rely on passwords, use passphrases instead. Passphrases are easier for you to remember but they're much harder to guess or hack than a word. You should make your passphrases random and avoid using your name or any other personal information about yourself.

Let's look at a few examples.

Passphrase Example 1: MonkeysDr3amInBananas!

Passphrase Example 2: MyPetIsOscar

The first passphrase (MonkeysDr3amInBananas!) is a great example of how to use a random passphrase that's easy for you to remember but would be very hard for a random stranger or hacker to guess or figure out.

Passphrase #2 is not as secure because it contains personal information that people might be able to obtain from your social channels, where you talk about your pet Oscar. That gives the hacker a place to start from. Making it a phrase does amp up the security, but it's only a matter of time before hackers start stringing together phrases with the information they're able to find about you.

Err on the side of random and nonsensical when you're setting up passphrases (and if it makes you laugh, that's an added bonus).

Browse Safely with HTTPS Sites Only

A useful way to tell if a site you're on is secure and trusted is to take a peek at the web address. You may be surprised to learn that the standard format of web addresses has changed slightly: "HTTP" is now "HTTPS" on sites that the browser has deemed secure. As you're browsing online, make sure you pay attention to the web addresses you're visiting. If you don't see the "HTTPS" in the address bar, holster that clicking finger and get off that site immediately.

Don't Save or Auto-Fill Passwords in Your Browser

The first time you log in to an online account in your browser, you're going to be asked a very important question that goes something like this: "Would you like this site to remember your password?" Your answer should always be "No" or "Never." When you save passwords in your browser or allow them to auto-fill, you're putting your privacy at risk. If a con is able to access your computer and open a browser, he'll have everything he needs to steal your information by visiting sites and using the stored password to log in. You need to remember your passwords, but your browser does not.

Keep Your Head in the Cloud Services You Use

The cloud has revolutionized how software functions, and you probably access a lot of cloud-powered programs in both your personal and work life. The cloud is extremely convenient, but you need to make sure that you're always mindful of maintaining your privacy when you work in the cloud by:

- Never storing highly sensitive or personal data in the cloud.
- Being selective about which cloud(s) you use.
- Securing your cloud access with a strong password or encryption.

Say No to Cookies

Thanks to recent GDPR legislation in the UK, online marketers are now required to add more transparency to how site visits, link clicks, and other online behavior can be used for marketing purposes. One of the requirements is that when someone visits a site for the first time, they must be given the choice about whether they want to use cookies on the site (as a refresher, cookies are an online tracking technology—the technology that makes that pair of shoes you're looking at on a retail site follow you to your social media channel). While this legislation is not yet in place on the federal level in the United States, most businesses with an international customer base are choosing to implement cookie permissions regardless. Additionally, action is also starting to take place at the state level in California to support consumer privacy and rights, and other states are expected to follow suit. This means you have a good opportunity to protect your online activity and privacy because whenever you visit a site, a box may appear asking you if you want to use cookies or not. Saying no prohibits the site from tracking your online behavior after you leave their site. The fewer sites and technology you have tracking your behavior online, the more secure your privacy will be.

Clear Your Cookies, Cache, and Browser History Often

While it is possible to say no to cookies on many sites you visit, the new legislation is not universal, and you're still going to be "cookied" as soon as you visit many sites, without a box asking if you want that or not. This is why it's a good idea to regularly clear your cookies, cache, and browser history. Doing so removes those cookies and also erases the history of the sites you have been visiting recently. If someone other than you is able to access your computer, she could probably find her way to a lot of your data simply by looking at where you have been online. Clearing cookies, cache, and browser history is easy to do—just follow these steps:

- Look for a gear or three-dot icon at the top right-hand side of your browser window, and click on it.
- Choose "History" from the drop-down menu that appears.
- You should see a list of your site visits appear, with the option to "clear browsing history." When you click it, there should also be boxes for cookies and cache checked so you can clean up your history, cache, and cookies in one step.

Be Stingy with Your Clicks

Links are practically designed to make you gravitate toward them with your clicking finger poised and ready. Hackers and other online swindlers are banking on click-conditioning because often all they need you to do to infect your computer, or gain unauthorized entry to your device and information, is make that one click. Here are some key ways you can be stingy with your clicks:

- Only click on links that you trust on secure websites and if it looks strange, out of place, or just makes you tilt your head and think, "Hmmm" then holster that clicking finger and stop yourself. It's not worth it to click through anything that looks strange or gives you a bad feeling.
- If a link is to another story or something you want to learn more about, start a new search in your browser and find reputable, secure, HTTPS pages that have the information you're looking for.
- This advice should be heeded on mobile devices as well. If you ever receive a link in a messaging app, a text message, or via email from someone you don't know, don't open it, don't click it, and delete it immediately.

Embrace the Peace (and Peace of Mind) of Blocking Ads

You're probably going to get a great deal of satisfaction from embracing this next tidbit of advice because if you're like most people, ads, pop-ups, and commercials all annoy you, and for good reason. They interrupt you. They take your attention away from where you (the owner of your attention) want it placed, often without your control or any warning. You wouldn't tolerate this kind of behavior from another human (at least not for very long if that person is older than five) and you don't have to put up with it on your devices and online. Your social media, email, and mobile accounts all have ad preferences that you can customize to choose things you don't want to see. You can even turn off ads entirely in some cases (but not all). If you're especially vexed by ads, then you can also get ad blocker software and run it on your computer. If any ads are trying to pop-up on sites you're using online, they'll be ensnared and stopped before you ever see them.

Make Sure Every Computer in Your Home Has a Firewall

A firewall is something that you probably have on your computer, something that you didn't even know was working to keep your computer (and all of your personal data you store on it or access with it) safe. A firewall is a piece of software that blocks any outside and unauthorized attempts to access any part of your computer, while still allowing you to send messages or access parts of your own computer or Wi-Fi. Most updated operating systems you'll run on your computer should offer you firewall protection. If you have an operating system that is one or two versions old though, it may be time to upgrade to the latest version to make sure you have all the most advanced firewall protections in place. Protecting one computer isn't enough. Every computer in your home should be running an updated operating system with the most recent firewall protection options in place.

Don't Get Reeled In by Phishers

Phishing is a tactic that scammers use to try to gain personal details about you or get access to your private accounts and data. They use a lure that will catch your attention, whether it's through an email, a text, or a chat message online, and will either try to convince you to give some kind of personal information or click a link. Some of the most common signs of phishing scams are:

- Suspicious combinations of name, email address, and domain in an email
- Messages sent with only a link (and a weird looking one at that)
- Emails asking you to log back into an account or system
- Emails or messages saying you've won something and the site needs more information to get you your prize
- Emails asking for help or money

The list continues to grow as scammers think of more ways to try and lure others in to providing personal information or clicking on a malicious link. Don't fall for anything that makes you think "This is weird…"—weird usually means scam.

Empower Your Privacy by Powering Down Devices

While staying connected always and no matter what or where is a convenience we have in our tech-powered lives, it also means that the window available to hackers to access our data is: always. If your devices are always powered on and always connected to the Wi-Fi, whether in your waking or sleeping hours, then you're exponentially increasing the risk that your privacy could be breached. All it would take is one hacker to breach your network, and they'd have all-access to your always-on life. You can diminish this chance by powering off your devices when you're not using them (or at the very least, disconnecting them from the Wi-Fi). By powering them down, you're not only giving yourself a rejuvenating break from screen life, but you're also decreasing the likelihood that your devices can be accessed remotely. Almost every device has to be on in order to be hacked, so power down those devices when you're not using them, and power-up your privacy protection.

Change Assigned Passwords Immediately

Any time that you sign up for a new account online, whether it's email, social media, banking, or otherwise, you should:

- Only use that password you're provided at the point of signing up to log in for the very first time.
- While you're logged in that first time, make sure that you go into the account settings and reset your password.
- If that option isn't available, then you can log out and go through the process of resetting your password that should be offered on every login page you access. Doing so will ensure that you have a safe start to using your online account.
- Update your password often to make sure you're keeping the private details you're entrusting to that account under virtual lock and key (i.e., a strong password that changes frequently).

Read Privacy Policies for Any Accounts, Profiles, or Purchases Online

It's time to be honest…do you actually read those privacy policies that pop-up when you're signing up for an online account, setting up a profile, or even making a purchase? If you're like the majority of people, you probably don't. I mean, it's written in fancy legalese language, that must mean it's there to protect you and someone has taken the time to watch out for you and account for your safety, right? While in an ideal world this would indeed be the case, it may be that a privacy policy doesn't always have your own privacy concerns fully covered. You should take the time to read through any privacy policy you accept. It is a contract and you're agreeing to the terms and giving up a good portion of your rights should you encounter issues while using whatever account or service you're signing up for. It could very well say, "We're going to log into your account and look at all your information and maybe sell some of it, okay?" Or to be accurate, in legalese it may read something more like, "Henceforth the platform named as such will hitherto have entry in accordance with rights deemed suitable to masquerade into the named account for reasons including but not limited to…" You get the point. Struggle through the terms and read it all. You are smart enough to understand it and spot risks to your privacy.

Password Protect Online Documents and Shared Files

Online documents and shared files can streamline your work tremendously, but you're also entrusting an Internet program with your work, your words, and your ideas. You should always password protect your shared online files and make sure that only the people you want to see your documents have access. This way, you'll be able to control who is accessing your private thoughts and work, while enjoying the benefits that are born of collaborating with others you do trust.

Be Cautious When Sharing Files Through Free Chat Programs

Free chat programs online are a great tool for staying connected with family and friends through chat and video calls, but you should make sure that you're never giving the program too much potential access to your life during the times you're not using that program. Follow these guidelines:

- Only give the chat platform access to your camera and microphone during your video calls, and turn them both off again when you're finished.
- Be very cautious about what files or photos you pass through the chat box. It's easy and convenient to drag and drop those items into the box to share with your friends, family, and colleagues, but they're just as easy to intercept as well.
- Never share account passwords, banking information, or other sensitive, personal information through the chat box. Chats are stored, and even if you delete the information from the chat, it's still somewhere in the system, in a corner marked "deleted," which hackers often know how to access.

Never Share Passwords on Public Wi-Fi

As a general rule, you should never share your account passwords with anyone, but if a trusted family member, friend, or a professional colleague needs access to an account of yours for reasons you feel are valid and nonthreatening to your privacy, then you should take special care to never share passwords via online channels. Never share passwords over a public Wi-Fi network, and only share passwords with people you trust. No matter how high your level of trust is, once you've shared a password, you can consider it dead. Once your account's served its purpose (by your permission), go ahead and change your password. You never know when a relationship can turn sour, and it's best that as few people as possible know the passwords to your sensitive accounts.

Encrypt Data Stored on USB Drives or SIM Cards

While the process behind encrypting data to keep it more secure and harder to access is complex in and of itself, using it to protect any data you store on your USB drives or SIM cards is really quite simple. In most instances, all you have to do is:

- Plug your USB drive into the proper port of your computer. Easy. Check.
- Load files as you planned. Check.
- Then, simply right-click on the USB icon on your computer and enable the encryption option, which should be available through most major operating systems. The data on your USB file will be encrypted, and it will now require a password or special access code for the files and data to be unlocked going forward.

It's very easy to lose USB drives, and encrypting the data on them just takes a couple of seconds. Time well spent to protect your personal data and files from any tampering or fraud should that little storage device get lost, stolen, or otherwise compromised.

Always Have a Back-Up Plan for Your Personal Information

You probably store a lot of your personal data, information, and work through online channels. If any of them were to be compromised, what would happen? Would you lose all your data too? Would you know how to get back to your data to protect it? The truth is that if a service goes down, or gets hacked and wiped clean, you will lose your data. You will likely need to replace much of it if it's compromised, but to protect yourself as best you can, you should always back up your files on a device other than your main computer. You can use an external hard drive that you only connect to for saving files, and then disconnect to keep your backup files as safe as possible as well. Endeavor to keep the information in online documents, accounts, or profiles free of personal details and private information such as account passwords and banking details in case that online program is ever hacked. Because then, that hacker is one step closer to picking your online locks and gaining entry to your personal details.

129

Declare a Weekly
Data Cleanup Day

At first, you'll be really good about keeping up with all your privacy protocols, but things get busy, life takes over, and suddenly your online data is a cluttered mess! And clutter attracts bad behavior online.

You should declare a weekly data cleanup day each week to:

- Delete emails that you don't need.
- Close any online accounts you're not using anymore.
- Make sure you don't have any unnecessary or unused apps or programs.
- Empty the trash bin on your desktop.

Doing this once a week shouldn't take very long, and you'll clean up the mess that could tempt and attract trouble from busybodies or online dumpster divers looking for details left to rot.

130

Sign Up for Free Credit Monitoring with Your Bank or Credit Card Company

There are many different credit monitoring options available online, and it can be confusing to sift through all the bureaus, scores, reports, and monitoring systems that you can access to determine which are the most secure and accurate. Most banks and credit card institutions are coming to the rescue though. You probably have access to free credit monitoring (with a reputable service who will show you reports from all the major bureaus) right now through your bank or credit card company. You can go into your local branch or even sign up online to have access to your credit scores and reports under the strong security of your bank. This is a great way to get free (and protected) access to a credit report you can use to monitor regularly.

Contact Credit Monitoring Bureaus (in Writing) to Prohibit Data Sharing

When you sign up for credit monitoring, you probably agreed somewhere in the terms and services that your information can be accessed by the system to make recommendations for credit repair solutions, credit cards that you may want to sign up for, etc. (See why it's important to read those policies?) While the credit bureaus should never share or sell your information for malicious intent, they do benefit from showing you offers you may like, which can cloud judgment or at the very least open you up to a barrage of preapproved credit card and loan offers (and you know how that junk mail siphon can impact your privacy). You can ensure that none of your data is accessed or shared in any capacity, for any reason, by contacting each of the three major bureaus in writing, strictly prohibiting them from sharing any of your data for any purpose.

- Equifax: www.equifax.com
- Experian: www.experian.com
- TransUnion: www.transunion.com

Monitor Your Credit Report Regularly and Look for Anything Suspicious

While it's not a quality to revere in hackers, they are very clever. They're also sneaky, so the chances are that you'll never know if your information has been compromised or stolen. However, one of the first places you'll be able to spot any fraudulent activity against you is in your credit report. You should monitor your credit reports regularly and keep a keen eye out for anything that doesn't make sense or look right to you.

- Is there a new line of credit on your report that you don't recognize?
- Have your balances gone up substantially and quickly?
- Did your score drop suddenly?

Scan all the details of your credit report often, because it can be an alarm system for fraud and give you a map to start tracking down the person who stole your data.

Disable Your Webcam When It's Not in Use (Plus a Nifty Tape Trick)

When you need the webcam, it just opens up and works. When you're done though, what happens? Does it turn off? Does it stay on, just go quiet, and wait until you need it again? The answer is closer to the latter, and unless you disable it, your webcam on your computer is technically always on and waiting for you to engage it for whatever video conference or conversation you're about to take part in. While this is convenient for you, the problem is that it is also ready and waiting for anyone else who's able to access your computer and engage the camera. If a hacker or a computer savvy prankster is able to breach your Wi-Fi network or gain access to your computer remotely, he can engage the webcam and use it to watch and listen to everything happening in the privacy of your home. You can avoid this situation by disabling your webcam whenever you're not using it (by visiting the settings of your computer or laptop) or unplugging your webcam if it's one that connects through a USB cord. However, an advanced hacker, should he gain access to your computer, will be able to turn the camera back on. Placing a piece of dark-colored electrical or duct tape over your webcam will completely obscure anything from your webcam's lens, so keep a roll handy in your laptop bag or computer desk. Hackers can do a lot of tricky and devious things, but they can't reach through your screen and remove that tape. See? Duct tape truly is for everything!

Don't Go Anywhere Online That You'd Be Embarrassed for Others to See

A good general rule of thumb you can use to safely guide your time online—and protect your privacy at the same time—is to stay away from any websites, profiles, or other places online that you'd be embarrassed to show your family, friends, or colleagues. This isn't about being proper or upholding whatever morals shape your life and your personality. It's not even necessarily about being or feeling ashamed—but it is all about protecting your privacy. The sites that you would visit that you'd never want others to see, whether they are adult-themed or emotionally or socially charged, may also present a higher risk to you and your devices you use to visit them. Sites like these often have an array of ads and pop-ups that will appear, and if you click on them (even to close them), you could be served a non-stop flood of other ads and windows that contain viruses trying to infect your computer. If your computer does get a virus, everything on it (including your personal information and everything you've been accessing online) will be exposed and open to a stranger whose intentions probably aren't exactly pure.

Trust Your Intuition

The more you learn about how to keep yourself safe online and protect your privacy while not giving up the conveniences that technology and the Internet bring into your life, the stronger your knowledge base will be for how to spot potential risks and get around them before anything hazardous comes your way. But there's also something else you should be paying attention to—that gut feeling you get about things in life, that sense you get when you just *know* something is going to happen, bad or good—your sixth sense. It goes by many names and descriptions, but what I'm referring to is… your intuition.

Pay close attention to your intuition and let it help guide you. If something looks odd to you or gives you pause, even if you can't explain why, then don't click on it. Don't ignore your intuition. Trust it and move on without clicking that risky link or responding to that text that just seems a bit weird. Listening to your intuition is never something you'll regret.

Always Protect Your Last Four

You've probably begun to notice some of the most sensitive numbers in your life (your social security number and credit or debit card numbers) are being shortened to just the last four digits: on receipts when you pay, on forms you're asked to fill out for a variety of reasons, or for validating your credit card when you call to speak with someone about your account. This has probably begun to condition you to think that this is the "safe" version of these private details in your life. If most of the number is redacted, are you still at risk should those last four numbers get into the wrong hands? The answer is still yes. Just because you're starting to see shortened or redacted versions of these important numbers in your life doesn't mean that they can't compromise your privacy. It will be harder, sure, but still not impossible, so it's simply a good idea to never provide the last four of your social security number or credit/debit card numbers in any kind of online form or over Wi-Fi.

137

Get Silly with Your Security Questions

What is your mother's maiden name?
What was your first pet's name?
What's the name of the street you grew up on?

Sounding familiar? Security questions were initially designed as a safeguard to protect your information by making you answer some question to log in or make any changes to data in your account. Things only you would know. Things you'd always be able to remember because they're tangible and often monumental pieces of your life. This seems like a good idea, in theory, right?

If you've ever posted memories on social media or filled out fun surveys online, then a lot of these questions could have answers floating around on the Internet, and hackers know just how to harness and use all that information to breach your account. You need to get silly with your security questions if you want them to work for you.

- Make up random words or nonsense streets or create fake details that you will use for answering security questions.
- Make sure that these words or things have nothing to do with you and could never be tied to your actual life.

Set Up a Junk Email Account

You can exercise great judgment in where you enter your email address and only enter it for things that look safe and legit. But the truth is that no matter how careful you are, you're going to get emails that you weren't counting on and don't want. Somewhere along the line, your email address may get sold or you may end up getting a spammy email with a virus. At best this will lead to an inbox filled with absolute junk and at worst, it could jeopardize the security of any personal details you have in your inbox. But you don't have to miss out on those great recipes or forgo signing up for a newsletter from your favorite blogger or company. Just create a separate email account (under a different name if you want to be a privacy protection ninja...and you should, you really should) and then use that address to sign up for the things you're interested in online. This way, if things go awry, this email address won't be tied to anything personal about you or contain emails with private information.

Never Shop on Public Wi-Fi

Online shopping and e-commerce have re-engineered how we shop and consume goods. We can find almost anything imaginable that we could want online, pay for it, and have it shipped right to our doorstep without ever having to leave the privacy of our homes! It's amazing and extremely convenient, but you need to stay steadfast to a major rule for safe online shopping to keep your privacy intact. Never shop on public Wi-Fi networks. These networks are open. Not only could there be, but there certainly are, lurkers perusing those open connections just waiting for someone to make a misstep and enter private information in a form or begin shopping online. Shopping on a public network can expose your credit card details, address, and any other personal information you use or access along the way as you're shopping. Only shop from trusted, password-protected Wi-Fi connections like the one in your home.

Keep Private Matters Like Taxes and Banking to Private, Secured Connections

Online shopping isn't the only personal online activity you should keep on a private, secure Internet network. You also likely do all your banking online. You probably prepare and file your taxes online. While this makes these processes much more streamlined and efficient for you, it also opens up some potential risks to the very private details you're looking at in your bank account or entering into tax forms. Only do taxes or banking on your own personal, password-protected Internet connection, and never use a public, open Wi-Fi network or even a shared network like the one at your office or school for private matters of this magnitude. You never know who's on open networks, so it's best to keep anything personal and private on your home connection only.

Use Caution in
Popular Searches

While it is a great luxury to find whatever you're searching for on-line, you must exercise a bit of caution in your online searches to keep your privacy secure and intact. Be careful in your more popular searches (beauty, fitness, celebrities, adult sites). This is malware's home base, and the results that you'll find may often be littered with ads or additional links to click within an article that will initiate a mal-ware invasion on your computer. Malware impacts the function of your computer and is usually a way that hackers can gain entry to your machine, and then your Wi-Fi and anything connected to or on your network. If an article is littered with ads, or you have to click through another link inside an article just to get to the information you're interested in, then you're clicking down a dangerous path.

142

Set Up a Browser Alert
for Your Name

A great way to keep an eye on where you're being mentioned or popping up online is to set up browser alerts for your name or the names of your children. This way, you'll receive a notification any time that your name is used online, which can help you see if there's anything coming up online about you that also includes private details. A large part of protecting your privacy is knowing what information exists and is living out in the wild on the Internet. If you can find it and harness it, you can tame it or get rid of it much more easily.

Use an Online Identity Monitoring Service

In addition to setting up a browser alert for your name, you can also explore the online identity or reputation management solutions available. These tools can be synced with social channels as well as other online media channels to notify you when your name is coming up all around the web or in social apps. This will help you get even more insight into where you're appearing online, so you can manage those places and ensure that your private information isn't among the things popping up around the web.

CHAPTER 5

How to Enjoy Social Media While Retaining Your Privacy

Social media is a force of nature. In just over a decade, it's progressed from a fun way to connect with long-lost friends and relatives to a major hub for communication, business, marketing, and more.

At the same time you have innovators endeavoring to change the world for good, a group of individuals looks at change and advancement as an opportunity to find system weaknesses and exploit them for fraudulent purposes. Social media offers these opportunities in spades because as a whole, people tend to share way more information than they should through social channels. While a large part of protecting your privacy on social media is rooted in taking full advantage of all the tools a platform has in place for you to shield your information, there are a multitude of ways you can compromise your privacy that have nothing to do with the actual social platform itself.

These privacy protection hacks will help you examine your behaviors in online social channels and give you insight into how you can enjoy your social time online without giving up critical components of your privacy.

Personalize Your Ad Preferences and Experiences

Social media platforms are no longer just for socializing. A host of businesses use social platforms to reach their customers and interact with them through posts, messages, and even advertisements. For you, as a social user, this means that you're now the target for ads—and a lot of them. While the social platforms monitor ads and have rules in place about the type of content, links, and subject matter that ads can contain, you can play a more active role in your ad experience by adjusting your preferences in your account settings.

You can choose what kinds of ads interest you and take a part in controlling the particular advertising that reaches you. Paying attention to your ad preferences will not only help limit ads, but it can help you sift out any inappropriate ads with adult content that slip through the cracks. Ads invite riff-raff, so always be careful what you're clicking through, no matter how reputable the platform you're using.

Keep Your Relationship Status Between You and Your Significant Other

Social media offers fields where you can declare the status of your love life and even tag your partner, boyfriend/girlfriend, spouse, or anyone else in your life you deem as your significant other. But it's better for your privacy protection goals to keep your relationship status and news to your trusted circle of friends, in person. Here's why:

- If you list your relationship status, then someone who's snooping on you to compromise your identity has just gotten another point of connection.
- If you've used your spouse's name as part of any of your passwords or use your anniversary as your PIN, then that snoop now has more information when trying to hack your passwords.
- The snoop can go on to your significant other's profile as well, and if he or she doesn't have privacy settings set up as strong as yours, it could give away even more information about your life together and the personal details you share as a couple.

These online snoops are on a twisted treasure hunt, and if they can collect enough information about you online, then they'll form a map that leads them to the treasure they're seeking: your identity, money, personal details, etc. So don't give them any hints.

Hide Your Friend List

It may feel good to show off all your friends and connections, and it may give you the feeling of popularity, influence, or clout, but it's also a privacy concern. This is probably something that you haven't considered, but even if you have your profile pretty privatized, your friends may not have the same measures in place. If someone is trying to gather information about you for any reason, if he hits any road-blocks, he can start looking at your friends' profiles. If your friends' profiles aren't strong on the privacy front, this snoop may be able to find photos of you or see where you're included in group check-ins and begin amassing more and more information about you that he can use for information hijacking. Think about how much someone could learn about your life and your habits from your friends. Does this risk seem a bit higher up in priorities than popularity? Hide your friends and contact lists on your social profiles to keep snoops from sniffing around your friends when they can't get a direct line to you.

Make All Your Photos and Albums Private

Social media can be used as a living, breathing scrapbook of your life as it unfolds. But, of course, there's always something that can ruin this wonderful way to share and connect. Photo sharing online is also another way you can compromise your privacy online. When you post your photos online, you're opening yourself up to the risk that someone who should not be looking at your photos certainly will. While someone lurking just to see your pics is creepy all in itself, clever hackers will be looking for whatever personal details they can gather from your pictures.

If you are going to post your photos online, make sure that you set all of your pictures and any albums you create to "private" so that only your friends can see your pictures.

Limit Access to Your Posts
(Even the Older Ones)

It's very much a natural inclination to want to share your life, and social media is the new medium many people now use to do it. But this also creates privacy risks because when you share intimate details of your life, heritage, and goals online, they're open for everyone to see. That's why you should take the time to control who can access your profiles and posts. You can set rules about how your posts are shown and to whom. This is a great way to fulfill that urge to keep a timeline of your life, while also making sure that none of your personal details leak into the wrong hands. When you're setting up your preferences on who can see your posts (which should be available to "just you" and "only friends" for optimal privacy results) don't forget about your old posts. Often, what will occur when you change your settings is they take place going forward, but it may be possible for someone to see old posts if you don't take care to apply your changes to all posts, past, present, and future.

149

Leave Groups or Parties Others Have Invited You to Without Your Permission

Social media groups are typically open to anyone, and it's also possible for your friends or contacts to add you to groups without your permission. A group owner can also add people to her group or party by perusing the list of friends of anyone already in the group. You'll become aware of this when you start seeing posts from a person or retailer you don't know.

If this happens to you (and it probably will), you should:

- Leave the group or party you've been added to immediately, particularly if you don't know the person whose posts are suddenly taking over your entire timeline. The risk here is that when you're added to an unknown group, your profile is now available to a sea of strangers; everyone in that group or looking at the group members can now see you. If you don't have your profile fully private, then you could have an array of strangers lurking and spying on your private details.
- You can also block the group as well to ensure that you don't get added again in the future.
- If it's friends or people you know, inform them that you are not interested in being added to any groups and ask that they refrain from ever adding you to any without your permission.

Put Controls in Place for Posts or Comments You Allow on Your Wall, Page, or Timeline

Even if you take the best measures to keep your profile and information private and are careful about the information you include in everything you post online, your friends and contacts will always be a bit of a wildcard. You won't know what they're going to say or what details about your life they'll reference in a post on your wall or timeline. Without meaning to be troublesome or compromise your privacy, a friend may post something that refers to personal details you want to keep private.

You can control what others post to your social media profiles by adjusting your settings so that any comments or posts your friends want to make on your wall, photos, or timeline have to come through you for approval. You'll receive a notification that someone wants to post a comment and you can review it to make sure it doesn't contain any personal details. This also protects you from spammy posts that hacked friends may mass post and it gives you complete control over what you'll allow on your social media for all to see.

Hide Your Personal Information (or Better Yet, Remove It Entirely)

Social profiles actually include a slew of private details about you in the "basic" information categories on the sites. There are fields where you can enter your email, phone number, birthdate, location, places you've worked, etc., and all those details will appear by default and be displayed prominently on your profile or page. These details won't just appear to your trusted friends and contacts you're connected with on social media; they'll show up as part of the information available when others do searches as well. So even if you have your profile set to be private and only visible to friends, anyone who comes across your name in a search can see these personal tidbits of information about you under your name and profile picture.

Some of the information is required for setting up a profile (such as email address), but you should remove any personal data from your profile (age, birthdate, location, etc.). Hiding it all will shield it from onlookers who are up to no good but should the social platform ever be victim to a data breach, your "hidden" information will once again be exposed since it's still part of the system even when it's "hidden." The ultimate hiding place for your personal details is off social media entirely.

152

Change Your Password Frequently

Social media accounts contain a lot of personal details and private information about your life. It's not unlikely that there'll always be a group of fraud-minded scammers out there who are trying to crack the code on your account to get into those personal details. To head them off and give them that extra hoop to jump through, change your password often. Every time your social media app runs an update or you see new features or cool new options being added to your profile, change your password and do a sweep of your privacy settings. System changes and updates are a time when hackers see if they can slip in unnoticed while things are happening in the system. Just for good measure, and for enhanced privacy protection, you should change your password often, even if you don't notice any changes. Remember, it's harder to hit a moving target, and this applies to hackers as well.

153

Notify Friends If Your Profile Goes Funky (You've Probably Been Hacked)

Your friends are suddenly messaging you or texting you asking what your rude social media message was all about. They're asking you why you tagged them (and forty-seven other people) in a flyer for discounted sunglasses. Parts of your profile have been changed or moved around. These are all signals that your social media account has been hacked. If you notice any of these signals, you should:

- Change your password immediately.
- Make sure your privacy settings are all up to date.
- Let everyone know that your profile was hacked and that was not you posting those ads or sending those messages. Suggest that they all change their passwords and beef up their security settings.

If the problem continues or personal data in your profile is missing or compromised, then you should get in touch with the social media platform immediately and deactivate your account until you have resolution on the matter.

Use Common Courtesy As Your Guideline for Information Sharing

As you're going about your socializing online, remember to be courteous to your friends and family, and do your very best to never expose anything private about their lives on social media (whether intentionally or accidentally). Before you post anything about illnesses, deaths, births, pregnancies, changes in job, moving, etc., you should always ask whether it's okay to share that information on his or her social media. You would never want anyone to blast your private details on social channels, so make sure you're not violating anyone else's privacy by sharing personal details.

155

Be Direct with Family and Friends about Maintaining Your Privacy

Just as you'd ask a friend or family member before posting about anything happening in their life in social media, expect your friends and kin to do the same by you. And don't just expect it and then be disappointed, embarrassed, or worse yet, violated; be upfront and clear about how you expect your personal information that's entrusted to others to be handled in online social settings.

Don't assume that your contacts know how you want them to behave, but tell them directly and specifically about the types of information you don't want them to share online, ever.

Keeping an open and direct dialogue going with your friends and family will help ensure that they know how to protect your privacy (and theirs) and that they don't accidentally share personal information online about you.

156

Avoid Info-Grubbing
Ploys on Social Media

Social media is also the perfect way for others to gather personal information about you under the guise of fun or by playing into your natural human curiosity.

For example, you can probably learn by navigating through some funny, clever charts, that if your birthdate is February 2nd, your donut name would be Frosted Twisty McTwister Buns.

Then you post your funny donut name in the comments...ha ha ha! But guess what you've just done? You've shared your birthdate on social media, which can be combined with other information on your profile (like your age, city where you live, etc.) to compromise your personal privacy.

Start looking at these games with a more critical eye, and really think about what information you're inadvertently giving in order to participate. If you want to play along but stay safe, just find the funniest name combo and post that. But avoid anything that is subtly asking you to share information, such as your birthdate, that can put your privacy at stake.

157

Turn Off Your Location in Your Social Profiles and Accounts

You can give away a lot of personal details about yourself by keeping location services turned on. The fact that it is always on means that anyone who is able to hack your social media account can gather location details about you, even if you didn't actually check in to those places. Online snoops don't deserve a play-by-play of your life and location.

158

Wait Until You're Back Home to Post Vacation Details and Photos

Aside from making your friends a tad jealous, there doesn't seem to be much wrong with posting your vacation photos and activities on social media, right? Unfortunately, there are scavengers who could use vacation posts as extra incentive to take a run at your home or try to get access to your personal data while you aren't paying attention to all the responsibilities of normal life. You can signal to crooks that your home is unattended or even send a sign to a lurker who's gotten hold of your credit card data and is waiting for an opportunity to make some purchases.

During a vacation, you probably aren't going to notice excess spending right away and you're not at home to make sure all your personal items and data are secured. That's what your tropical photos will show devious plotters. Save those photos until you get home and then post them in a private album for just your close friends and family to enjoy as you tell them tales of your trip. A story you don't want in that collection of vacation memories is how your privacy was jeopardized while you were away.

159

Don't Share Photos of Your Children in the Bath, Nude, or in Other Embarrassing Situations

Do you have any bath time, naked, or otherwise private and embarrassing photos that your parents loved to share or your siblings tormented you with? Most of us probably do. But the thing that's changed is that a photo on social media is not just seen by your mom's friends while they're having brunch with her. It has the potential to get onto all kinds of screens in no time at all. Preserve your memories, but make sure that you're not posting private pictures of your children online when they cannot or don't consent. Even though there's not much more adorable than a baby picture, invading your child's privacy isn't cute at all.

Don't Give Away Your Children's Identity with Their Birth Details

When your precious baby finally arrives, you're understandably going to be very excited to announce her birth and let all your friends know that the delivery went well and everyone's doing fine. However, you should avoid posting your newborn child's full birth details via social media. It's a very common practice to share a baby's date of birth, where she was born, how much she weighed, how many inches long she is, her full, legal name, and so on. You get the point. These are all details that you, as a proud parent, want to share to give some shape to who this precious little bundle is. But what you're also doing is putting private details online that could give fraudsters just enough info to start trying to hustle up credit cards or set up utilities in your baby's name. This kind of thing can go on for years. Keep birth details off social media and only share them in person with trusted friends and family.

Create Private Photo Albums Just for Family and Selected Friends

To keep your privacy intact, you need to be very careful about what photos you share online and who has access to see them. Without realizing it, you can give away little clues about your life and your personal information in the photos you share. For example, you may want to share a photo of your fabulous kitchen remodel. What you don't notice is that there's a stack of mail on your countertop. It's little things like this that data prowlers are looking for online by sifting through any photos they can click on. There are clues and pieces of your personal data all around you as part of the landscape of your life, and you may not even notice they're in a picture. But people who're looking for just that kind of information will know how to look for those things you're not noticing, and they'll know how to use them in conjunction with other data they may have to put your privacy and personal information at risk. You can set up private photo albums on your social media accounts and only make the photos you share there open to a group of friends and family. This way no one can find your pictures from your profile or get them to come up in their searches online. Protect the precious life moments you capture in pictures—they're yours, after all.

Keep Your Address Out of Your Online Photos

Setting up private photo albums on your social media accounts and staying mindful about every item that is in the pictures you post (private or not) are steps you can take to enjoy sharing pictures from your life with friends online while protecting your private data. However, one more important piece of information that can end up in your photos (again, without you even thinking about it) is your home address. You may post a picture that has a piece of mail on the counter, which shows your home address. Or you may post a picture of your new landscaping in the front yard that shows the number on your house. You may post a picture of your kids on their first day of school, standing in front of your home, which again, shows your house number. These are all things worth photographing, celebrating, and sharing with your loved ones and those close to you, but they're also the clues that online snoops are looking for to get just one more piece of your data. Additionally, if the social platforms you use are ever breached, these are the kind of little things fraudulent snoops will be looking for to compromise your personal information.

Beware of "Too Good to Be True" Syndrome

In and of itself, the Internet sometimes seems too good to be true, and it makes anything seem possible. The same types of insane offers you'd scoff at elsewhere you may look at on social media channels and think maybe, just *maybe* this *is* real.

The opposite is true. The sweepstakes, the surveys, the chances to win a new car, a free $100 gift card, a new phone or tablet (for *free!*), and notifications you've won a grand prize (in a drawing you never entered) are all just different ways to grab your attention and get you to provide some kind of information. It may be a company wanting to get you on their mailing list, but it may be someone with more sinister plans for your personal data. When it comes to offers such as these, the age-old adage has not changed:

"If you see something online that is too good to be true, it most certainly, definitely, without question *is*."

Remember: Online Posts Have a Very Long Shelf Life

Everything you post online to your social channels (even if you're careful with what you say and are diligent about maintaining good privacy health in your account settings) has the potential to live in infamy online. Even if your posts are hidden or blocked from certain individuals, every piece of data you enter and everything you share is preserved in the social media platform's information database. This means that a wayward or disgruntled employee of the social platform could misuse or sneak away with your personal information. It means any type of breach suffered by the platform can expose the information you thought was private.

It's important to remember that nothing you post online can ever be truly private; it's always going to be somewhere in a database waiting to be discovered. The best way to protect yourself is to never post any private or sensitive information on social channels.

Be Cautious about Profile Sharing on Any of Your Social Professional Accounts

Social channels continue to evolve as people figure out more creative ways to connect online for personal and professional reasons. Some of these channels have an option where you can share contacts or profiles, which means that your profile can also be shared by others. Now, if you're job hunting, or you're looking to connect with more professionals in your niche, this can be a great way for you to get exposure or get your information into the right hands to make that next big career move happen for you. However, there are swindlers and crooks who are counting on career motivations clouding your judgment. You should be very careful about the information you have included on your professional profile, and make sure that it's information you wouldn't mind strangers having. However, it's much better for your privacy if you turn off the profile-sharing feature in professional accounts, so that your details cannot be passed to or seen by strangers. No matter how hungry you are for your next opportunity, there may be someone hungrier for your personal information.

Don't Share Data with Third-Party Apps

You should always be cautious of clicking through any ads you may see on social channels (and any pages or articles your friends share on their feeds). They could be attempts to get you to download or interact with a third-party app. The most reputable places to find verified apps is through the major app stores offered by your device provider. These apps are vetted and held to a standard designed to keep users safe.

However, there are also a lot of third-party app creators out there who don't list their apps in a verified store. Instead, they try to get information or downloads through other social media channels. This is a huge red flag. Third-party apps are more likely to contain viruses or malware, which will put your personal privacy at risk the moment you download the app, enter your personal details, or share your social profile data to gain access to an app, article, survey results, etc.

If you see an app you're really interested in appear in ad format, jot down the name of the app and then search it in the app store offered by your phone provider. Taking this extra step will help you avoid falling into third-party app traps, which may be ploys to get your personal information or access to your devices.

Practice Conscious Sharing

Part of keeping your privacy safe (whether it's karma or just being a good online citizen) is monitoring what you share (and who you share it with). Here's how you can be a conscious sharer:

- Be mindful about the things you share and make sure that the posts don't link to questionable articles, which spammers use to mine data away from people under the guise of learning or reading more.
- Don't share anything containing private or personal information about your friends. Practicing good privacy protection means taking care of your own personal data, but it also calls on you not to expose the personal details of others.

Block Anyone You Don't Want to Connect with Professionally

You should be cautious about who you choose to network with on professional connection sites. While you can find legitimate opportunities and collaborate with other professionals in your niche, or even peruse for your next big career move, there are people out there whose business *is* fraud. Before you accept an invitation to connect from someone you don't know, do your research.

- You can start by checking out his profile, but keep in mind that he could have fake information that looks professional just to lure you into providing personal information he says is required to vet you for a new job.
- Before you even embark on connecting with a new professional contact, search him online.
- Research the company he says he's with and see if you can find any reviews or credible business accreditations.
- Look for the person in the "Team" section of the company website. If he's claiming to be an executive or someone in charge of hiring, he'll most likely be listed here.

Taking these extra steps to vet a person can give you confidence you're dealing with a real person with a real opportunity for you.

Control Who Can Message You on Social Platforms

Social media messaging is one of the common places in which a hacker will try to get you hooked. If you notice messages from people you don't know, delete them. Don't be tempted to open them, but if curiosity gets the better of you and you do so, never click on any links or fall for claims that someone has found a salacious photo or video of you that they're saying you should know about. Hackers can infiltrate your profile if they can get you to click on a link or a fake file infected with a worm or a virus, which will go to work quickly and get them access to your profile and probably much of the other personal data you have on your computer, phone, or any other device connected to your Wi-Fi. If this happens, report the person immediately and block him from sending you messages. But you can remove this worry entirely (at least from strangers) by blocking anyone who's not your friend on social media from sending you messages. This way, a fraud-intending con has no way of sending you those wormy messages or virus-ridden video clips in the first place. You can minimize the risk to your personal privacy substantially by only allowing the people in your approved circle of social trust to message you.

170

Beware of the Social Media Survey

"What's the name of the street you grew up on?"
"Who was your favorite teacher?"
"What was your first car?"
"What was your first pet's name?"

Guess what this kind of information (playfully asked for in social media surveys) is commonly used for? Secret account security questions you need to answer to reset your password or gain access to your private online accounts. By filling out the survey and posting it on your wall you are practically hand-delivering answers to account security questions to those who are perusing social media just waiting for such a golden ticket.

You should avoid filling out surveys that ask you for personal details that may also be a gateway into your online account. As a good friend, pass along your concerns to your friend who posted that survey in the first place to warn her about the risks hiding in the seemingly harmless fun in social media.

171

Never Send Money via Social Channels

You've probably noticed a new icon in your social media channels, which—when you hover over it—indicates you can now send money to others you're connected with. Stay far away from this feature! While it may seem convenient to pay for an item you want to buy in the classifieds group or send your friend some money for picking up the dinner tab last night, think about what you're really doing. You're pumping your banking or credit card information right into the veins of social media, where it will live among all your other personal details when the next data breach occurs.

172

And Don't Send Money via Chat Apps Either

While we're on the subject, you should never send money through your chat programs either. Just because that option is now available to you does not mean that it's a safe way to send money to your contacts. Chat programs are regularly targeted by hackers because they're relatively easy to infiltrate and use as a vehicle for viruses and malware. Don't be tempted to do it once just to check it out. If you do, then your payment details are now part of the data contained in that chat program. If someone were to get into your chat program, he could easily clean out your bank account by sending himself money via your chat program.

CHAPTER 6

Strategies for Protecting Yourself and Your Privacy in Email, Online Classifieds, and Online Dating

The Internet provides ample opportunities to connect with others, for a variety of very different reasons or motivations. You can stay in touch with work colleagues, friends, and family members quickly and easily through email. You can peruse items for sale, look for upcoming yard sales, and find your next great deal on the online classifieds.

But where the Internet gives, it also has the potential to take away. While email, online classifieds, and online dating can add convenience, fun, and pleasure to your life, they are also places where con artists perpetuate fraud or try to get hold of your private details when you are off guard or not paying close attention. Some of their tactics are so subtle you may not notice them unless you know exactly where to look and what to watch for. Others may be more obvious and bumbling and easier to spot.

These privacy protection hacks will help you navigate the privacy risks inherent in email, online classifieds, and online dating so you can enjoy these activities and keep your personal information private.

173

Choose a Reputable Email Provider

Your inbox is a major hub of communication in your life, so you should make sure that the email provider you're using (whether at work or personally at home) is reputable and has all the latest technology in place to protect your personal data and information that is contained in your emails. There are several major companies that offer free email services, so you should make sure that you're using an email system that is not just popular, but current and relevant. (Hint: stick with established companies such as Google, Apple, and Microsoft, and avoid more antiquated ones like Hotmail and AOL.) These are the companies that lead the way in online innovation and system security, so your email is going to not only function more seamlessly but also have all the most updated spam filters and other protection technologies in place.

Remember, choosing a reputable email provider is certainly a best practice for keeping your private information safe while you're writing, sending, and saving emails, but it's not a complete fail-safe. You still need to exercise good judgment about what kinds of information you let in and out of your inbox. Common sense and a reputable email provider are a power duo for using email safely and keeping your private details private.

174

Use a VPN to Protect Remote Connections

Using a Virtual Private Network (VPN) is a great way to securely connect to systems and programs that run in the cloud or as part of a larger, highly secured network (such as at your office or place of work). You set up a login, and in order to verify you as a user, you have to use a code that appears on a key fob (and regenerates every couple of seconds to enhance security). You only have a few seconds to log in using a VPN, which helps ensure that you have the key fob and are an authorized user. If you're using a VPN for work or private home connections, take care to keep your key fob on your person. While's it a token of high security, it's a key part of what someone would need to access your entire private network.

175

There's *No* Nigerian Prince (and Other Email Scams to Avoid)

You've received an email announcing that you're the benefactor of a Nigerian prince's fortune! Millions of dollars in wealth are now yours. Even though you didn't know you had a prince in the family and have no idea how you've come into a fortune, here's a formal email announcing it. All you have to do is provide every bit of your personal information (for the paperwork, you know).

This is a very well-known email phishing scam where someone (decidedly not a prince) is trying to trick naïve email users into providing all their personal details for the mere chance that this huge wealth could be theirs. While it's well-known and reported, this scam still makes the rounds through inboxes every day, which means it must still be swindling some people.

While you may know to avoid this particular scam, it's birthed an array of copycat emails in which you're asked to provide personal information in exchange for a large sum of money or something very valuable. While the email may tickle your curiosity (despite being savvy and knowing you should never send personal details to a stranger) there is about a one in a million chance that any email offering you an incredible fortune (just give me your details!) is legitimate. When you get these emails, delete them. If you do have a prince in the family, and you're the heir to his fortune, you'll be notified through very formal channels, not through a poorly written email.

The IRS Doesn't Do Email

No matter what gives you pause about taxes, it's that pause that opens up a doorway for cons to get around your normally keen judgment. The most common email scam (that still floats around each year around tax season, no matter how much news coverage it gets) is one where someone (*not* the IRS) sends out emails posing as an IRS agent. These emails (and even phone calls) are usually fear-based, stating you owe the IRS money or that you're in danger of being imprisoned pretty much immediately if you don't provide payment. If you get an email with anything about the IRS in the subject line, delete it. The IRS themselves has put out many statements saying they will never email anyone. If you get a call, ask the "IRS agent" for her identification number. Every federal employee has one. If she cannot provide one, hang up and block her calls. If she does, call the IRS and let them know you've been contacted and ask them to verify the employee identification number you were given.

Much like princes, the IRS is going to use legal and very formal channels to contact you if they need to speak with you about your taxes. They will never email you and they certainly won't threaten you with impending arrest if you don't immediately wire them money or get them thousands of dollars in gift cards. You can't pay the IRS in gift cards, folks.

Beware of Any Emails Declaring You a Winner

If you receive emails from a person or establishment you're not familiar with saying that you've won a prize or a free gift, proceed with caution and a high amount of skepticism. Typically, these types of emails aren't actually offering you anything of value. Instead, they're trying to get your attention and see if you're willing to give up your personal information in exchange for the chance at maybe winning something: a trip, a free gift card, cash, etc. If (against your better judgment) you decide to enter your details, you'll probably find yourself spiraling down a rabbit hole of forms you need to fill out requiring more and different details. This is a dangerous hole because, in addition to providing way too much personal information, you're also likely to set off a trip wire on a virus that will compromise all your personal data on your computer or mobile device. Deleting these emails and protecting your private details is what will really make you a winner.

178

Know How to Spot (and Avoid) Ransomware Risks

When you get ransomware on your computer, all of your files will become inaccessible, your computer will freeze, and then a box will appear on your screen with a message about how much money you need to pay (and by when) to gain access to your files once more. The most alarming thing about ransomware is that it's always changing and the hackers using it are usually completely untraceable. There are no set, standard protections in place to defend you against ransomware as there are with other malware or viruses. The hacker is next to impossible to trace or locate, and there's no other choice but to pay the absurd fee they're asking for, or completely wipe your hard drive. Either way, all the personal information that was on your computer has now been breached (even if you pay to get it back).

Cons who use ransomware are clever in all the worst ways. The email they send and the files they want you to download usually look legitimate and may correspond to something going on in your life (yes, this means that the hacker's been spying on you for a while). You have to look closely—there will be a clue that something isn't right. The information will be too vague or the file will be named somewhat generically. Keep your fraud radar up and your click finger holstered to avoid getting taken for ransom.

Be Skeptical of Emails Requesting You "Log Back In"

If you're changing your password regularly (as you should be), then you've probably grown accustomed to the emails that come in to help you validate your password. They usually contain a code that you need to log back in so you can update your password. If you've initiated a password change, these types of emails are safe and helpful.

However, there are scammers who borrow formats from these emails and rely on your conditioning to follow the directions to get back into your account. A new wave of scam emails is now out there. These emails may even bear the name of an account, platform, or institution that you use. It falsely informs you that you need to get into your account for one reason or another. You should never follow instructions in an email that asks you to click through a link and then to log in to any account you own. In this scam, a con artist is trying to trick you into believing you need to "log back in" to your account, but what he's going to do is capture your login details once you've clicked through that link and entered them into the fields.

Reputable platforms and institutions such as your bank will never send you an email asking you to log back in. If you do receive an email like this, you should call the institution the email claims to be from and report it. Block the sender and delete the email, then change your password for good measure.

180

If You Don't Know the Sender, Delete the Email

One of the best habits you can get into for maintaining your privacy while using email is to delete any emails coming from a person, organization, or company you don't know anything about. Email is a popular vehicle for scams and viruses, and you can avoid a lot of privacy risks, keep your sanity intact, and eliminate clutter in your inbox by dumping any unknown emails into the trash. If someone you do know is trying to contact you, they will keep trying and will likely have other ways of reaching you rather than email. Taking this simple step will eliminate a lot of the incoming privacy concerns that may be hitting your inbox and phishing for information, and it will be liberating to work with a fresh, safe inbox.

Never Open Attachments or Zip Files from Unknown Senders

An attachment on an email has the same kind of effect as a wrapped gift. Even if it's not for you, and it's not your birthday or a holiday, when you see a beautifully packaged gift box (or email attachment), you want to open it up and see what's inside. Scammers exploit this natural curiosity by hiding viruses, malware, and ransomware inside attachments. They know that many people will not be able to resist seeing what's inside the attachment, even if they don't know the sender or have any reason to think the attachment holds anything they need.

Resist the urge to open any types of attachments on emails from unknown senders. At the moment, zip files are especially problematic because they can hold a lot of compressed data, making them perfect for housing ransomware. If you see an email from someone you don't know and can tell it has an attachment, delete the email and block the sender. Resist your natural curiosity and don't even open the email. All you have to do is click on that file for the devastation of your privacy to begin so you can remove this temptation (and salvage your private information from pilfering) by deleting that email and moving on.

Mark Unwanted Email As Spam

Despite your best efforts, you're probably still going to receive emails that you don't want to receive. If you receive an email that seems suspicious, then you can mark it as spam. This will trigger your spam filter to that address and it will move any emails from that address right to your spam box (rather than your inbox). You can also use this tactic for emails that keep coming no matter how many times you've tried to unsubscribe. If the sender of the email isn't respecting your wishes to stop receiving emails, then he may be just as persistent in his efforts to scam you out of your personal data. Marking these emails as spam flags the email address and sends a report to your email provider. If they get frequent spam hits on that address, it will be blocked from sending emails not only to you but to anyone who uses your email provider as well.

Dump Your Spam Box Daily

If you're using a reputable, established email provider then you should have a spam filter on your inbox. This technology helps by sifting through all the emails that are sent to your address and filtering out any that resemble past or current spam email trends. Spam filters are intended to protect you by doing some of the work of weeding through emails for you, and while the science isn't perfect, it's very valuable and will help you avoid a lot of spam emails.

However, it's not wise to just let those spam emails sit in the spam folder unattended. Your email provider will automatically delete any spam messages after a specified period, but whenever you're in your inbox each day, take a couple of seconds to dump the spam box and delete those emails forever. Spammy emails can be dangerous to your privacy if they're so much as clicked on or opened, so cleaning out the spam folder each day reduces the risk this will ever happen.

Ignore (and Delete)
Crisis-Based Emails

"You must act now, or legal action may be taken!"
"You'll be arrested today if you don't pay your debt!"
"Log back in now or your bank account will be closed!"

Another calling card of emails that harbor spammy intentions or are trying to gather your data is if they present you with a situation that scares you or creates a false crisis or sense of urgency. If you're acting in haste to avoid a very unpleasing result, you may not take the time to carefully think and examine the facts and look closely at the email. At least, that's what cons dream about at night.

Rest assured, anything of the magnitude being threatened by these emails will never come to you out of the blue; news of this nature doesn't come by email. However, by stirring up a fake crisis, scammers have been able to get information or even money from people who believe that some dastardly fate awaits them if they don't comply. If you receive any crisis-based emails, remember that it's just a disguise, a scary mask that someone is wearing to try and "boo!" you out of your personal information or money. Don't panic and never respond. Just block the sender, mark the email as spam, and delete it from your inbox.

Be Wary of Emails Asking for Help

In addition to false crises, email scammers may also try to pull your heartstrings or appeal to your helpful nature by sending emails asking for help. They can be clever and sometimes emails may even come under the name of a friend or family member. If you receive an email asking for help, the best thing you can do is contact your friend and ask about the email. She may have been a victim of a privacy breach as well, so she does need your help after all.

Watch for Emails from Names You Know (but Look or Feel "Off")

Typically, scam emails, when they come from a familiar name or organization, will have at least one of these key calling cards to alert you that a scammer is truly behind the email. You can identify these emails quickly by asking yourself the following questions:

- Is your friend's name spelled wrong?
- Is your "friend" asking for help using a different email than she normally uses?
- Does the email only contain a first name (whereas emails from that friend normally come under a first and last name)?
- Does the domain name look suspicious or unfamiliar?

If you answered yes to any of these questions, it's a scam email. You should let the friend whose name was used know about the email and suggest she change her passwords and look into her privacy health. Then delete that email and block the sender.

Use Reverse Image Search to Validate Photos in Online Classified Ads

As great as online classifieds can be, they also tend to attract a lot of fraud. One of the fastest ways you can spot a scam in the classifieds is to be skeptical. Remember how anything too good to be true online most definitely is? This applies to the classifieds as well (if not more). If the photos look airbrushed or too good to be true, you can put your suspicions (and your hope) to rest by saving that photo and plugging it into a reverse image search on your browser. You'll probably find it on another site, in its original, unaltered form. Classifieds scammers exploit the desire for a good deal and will often simply steal photos from a current listing and post an ad of their own, at a much lower price, to see if they can get people to give them information through a fake application or put down a deposit.

Look for Typos, Spelling and Grammar Errors, or Odd Characters and Text in Online Classifieds Ads

Another trick you can use to spot potentially scam-ridden classifieds ads online is to pay attention to how the ad is written. Are there a lot of spelling and grammar mistakes that make it hard to understand? Are there a lot of typos or odd punctuation marks in the middle of words? You're probably not going to find ads with eloquent prose and impeccable grammar in the classifieds, but you should be able to understand the details being listed. If you can't, there's a good chance the ad is fake and just being used for information gathering. You should also avoid any ads that have excess punctuation marks or symbols scattered in random places in the text (particularly if the ad suggests you click on a link to learn more, see more pictures, etc.). You should avoid clicking on any links in classifieds ads in general, but especially steer clear of those that are in ads along with weird characters and symbols.

Give Preference to Online Classifieds Listings with a Phone Number (Preferably Local)

The most prevalent type of scam that you'll find on any online classifieds site or group is one where an ad seems like a great deal, with a price that's just a little too low. It may also only list an email address to contact someone about the item you'd like to buy. Now, there could very well be exceptions here. Someone may be at work when he posts the ad and prefers to just manage emails (and not phone calls) over the course of the day. But if there's an email address only, you should be a little suspicious. If you do decide to email that person about the item for sale, do it through one of your alternate email addresses that you've set up, under a fake name and information. If it's a scam, the scammer is going to reply with an email that may blatantly ask you for very personal information or he may try to take you through a link. Either way, you don't want anything suspicious coming through your personal email in case it's a scam and the email is the vehicle. By emailing the poster, you're consenting to communicate, so be very cautious about ads that look weird and just have an email address or link for contact. Ads with real pictures that show imperfections, written in easy-to-understand language, with a local phone number are generally the most trustworthy ads.

Beware of Texting Scams
Initiated in Online Classifieds

Texting is often a preferred mode of communicating about deals listed on online classifieds sites (for both the seller and the buyer). It's quick and easy, and you don't have to endure awkward silences as you try to remember the questions you wanted to ask about the item you're interested in buying.

However, because texting is so popular and convenient, it's also been picked up by scam artists as a way to mislead or swindle classifieds shoppers. You should never provide any personal information to a stranger via text. Keep the conversation strictly on the item for sale and never give out your name, email, address, or any other personal or payment information via text. If you're sent a link via text, do not click on it. It's most likely an attempt to gather your personal details, or worse yet, hack your mobile device with a virus or a worm.

Use a Secure Email Service When Selling Items on a Classifieds Site

When you list your items for sale online, you're likely going to be signing up for an onslaught of emails, phone calls, and texts from strangers, so you need to make sure you're being smart and protecting your private information as much as possible in these exchanges. If you've set up alternate phone numbers that you can forward to your mobile, then it's prudent to use that number so you don't expose your real number online. You can also use that alternate email address you've set up for junk mail to communicate with potential shoppers.

If you're using an established online classifieds site to sell items that you no longer need, you also have the option to use a secure emailing system that shields your real email address and allows you to interact with people without exposing your real email address. You'll be given an address by the platform that's random but forwards to your inbox. Keep in mind though, as a buyer, when you use the emailing service, your name and email come through to the seller just as if you'd emailed them directly.

Be Cautious about Switching Communication Mediums During a Classifieds Conversation

While online classifieds can be a great source for finding a good deal or scoring a really unique item you'd probably never find new in a store for the price, they also attract a lot of fraud and scams. Listening to your intuition will often help guide your decisions on whether or not to engage in a conversation about an item you're interested in, and as a general rule, you should avoid even starting a conversation about an item that is simply too good to be true.

But there are great (and legitimate) deals, and you can find them and interact safely if you know how to avoid communication swaps that are likely a ploy for your personal details or your permission (in a very roundabout way) to email you. You may get a response (maybe with a backstory—the most common one of late is someone selling an item for her mother) saying that you should provide your email to get more details about the item you're interested in buying. Think about this for a minute: your name and email already came through, and you're already conversing; why would you need to provide your email? Because then the person you're talking to has permission to contact you at that address and it's all in writing in your email exchange. If you fall for this, you're probably going to receive a lengthy email that requires you to either provide information or maybe even a deposit before you've even seen the on-sale item.

Never Pay for an Item You Haven't Seen in Person

You should never pay any amount (through any method) for anything you haven't seen and validated in person. While this may seem obvious, crooks are clever, and they know how to play to your emotions and make you feel like you may lose your chance at what you want to buy if you don't act quickly. For example, many people peruse the online classifieds to look for a new home or apartment rental. If you live in a city where rentals fill up quickly, then you may find yourself in a frantic search. Criminals follow trends and patterns and they'll often post duplicate (and completely fake) ads that contain pictures and information about a place that isn't even for rent. They play on your desire to move quickly and may ask you to fill out a form in advance or even put down a deposit before you've set foot in the rental in question. Be patient and don't react to this false urgency. It will typically just end up with you exposing your private details, perhaps even losing money, and at the end of it, you'll still not have a place to call home. Always pay for items in cash and never trust any ad that requires you send information or payment in advance of seeing an item, apartment, or anything else in real life.

Don't Display Your Home Address in Any Ads You Post to the Classifieds

One of the best ways to get the word out about your yard sale is through your local online classifieds group on social media or in the bigger online classifieds sites for your city or area. However, you should be cautious about how you provide the personal information people will need to find your big sale. You certainly don't want your home address floating around online in social media or classifieds sites, so you should never list your home address in your ad. Instead, list your nearest cross streets and give vague directions by saying something like "Located just past the intersection of Main St. and Broadway Dr. Follow the signs!" This will get people in your general neighborhood and then you can make some bright signs to help people find their way to the new treasures they want to take home (without risking your privacy in the process).

Don't Use Photos That Display Personal Details

Classifieds listings with photos will get the most attention, so if you want to sell items quickly you should use photos. However, take care that you're never including pictures in your ads that have private details in them or in the background. Follow these guidelines:

- If you're selling a car, don't include a photo that shows the license plate.
- If you're selling a desk, make sure that your computer screen isn't on or that there aren't any bills or other private documents on the desk.
- If you're selling some outdoor planters, make sure that your home number isn't in the background of the photos.
- Don't use a picture of a closet organizer that shows the location of the safe or lockbox you keep in the closet.

You get the idea. Start thinking about every personal bit of information that someone might be able to glean from the photos you want to use. Even if it means you have to retake some photos, it's time well spent to keep your privacy intact (and get those items sold).

Never Show Items for Sale Inside Your Home

While you should generally try to meet people in a neutral, public location to sell a classifieds item, there may be times when you're selling something very large and heavy that doesn't make sense to transport to a public, neutral location. In these very rare instances, you may have to show an item at (but not inside) your home. Doing these key things will help you keep your privacy as safe as possible:

- Bring the item outside or into the garage to show it in your yard to the interested buyers.
- If you have a few people interested, schedule them to come in ten- or fifteen-minute intervals.
- If no one buys the item, move it back into your home or garage. This is a little extra effort, but it will ensure that people who are coming in to see an item are not actually trying to gather up personal information about you or your home.
- You should also only provide your address when you know the person is on his or her way. Ask for a phone number and then call the prospective buyer to give directions as he or she is about to leave.

Leave Your Family and Pets Out of Classifieds Photos

Just as you would not include any personal details in the photos you're using in online classifieds ads, you should also avoid getting your family or pets in the photos as well. Whenever you post a photo anywhere online, you are putting it into an endless library of images that others can easily get their hands on (whether they're advanced hackers or just the normal bumbling browser user). Take care not to put any photos of yourself and your family into classifieds sites, where there are no privacy settings for you to control who can see or download your photos. For example, if you're selling a high chair, don't use a picture that has your baby in the chair. Take the extra time to take a photo of it by itself. If you're taking a photo of a mirror you're selling, it might be a bit trickier, but with a little positioning, you should be able to get a nice photo of the mirror without any reflections of your family or any private area of your home.

198

Read the Classifieds Rules As Inspiration (and Follow Them Too, Of Course)

You should read the rules of any group you join or any site you post on (yes, so you don't get kicked out for inadvertently breaking the rules) but also to get an idea of how the group is set up (or isn't) to protect your privacy as a group member. Most social classifieds groups should have an admin, so if you have any concerns about how your privacy is maintained, you can message that person for help. Along with beefing up your privacy settings on your profiles, you should make sure the group is safe and that old posts are deleted regularly in the group. Getting a little nerdy upfront can help you understand how the site or group works, which will help you decide if it's a safe place where you can maintain as much anonymity as possible as you peddle your goods.

199

Know How to Validate Online Dating Profiles

By their nature, online dating sites and apps ask for a lot of details about you, your personality, and your life. The intention, of course, is to help you find people you'll be compatible with and narrow your search to determine who you'll go on a date with in real life. However, because online dating is so rich in personal details, it's also an activity that can put your personal information at risk. A fraudster on the platform may try to trick you out of personal details. Such a person has no intention of meeting you, but she may try to temporarily become you by assuming parts of your identity. Scammers on dating sites will try to allow your emotions to carry you away; in such circumstances, you may overshare your personal information.

You should be very cautious about the people you choose to interact with on dating sites. Keep your intuition turned on high and if anything gives you pause, go the other way. If someone seems nice but is trying to get too personal too quickly (asking you specifics about your life, where you live, where you work, if you live alone, etc.) then that person may not actually be trying to make a connection; rather, she is trying to get as much personal information as possible.

Know How to Spot Catfishing Ploys on Dating Sites

To keep your privacy intact and find your chance at love online, you should know how to spot profiles that probably aren't actual people looking for romance. Profiles are easy to set up and you can enter anything about yourself that you want. Crooks looking to scam the lovelorn can set up fake profiles to lure people in, gain their trust, and gather personal information about them under a guise. This is called catfishing, and it's happened to many people under different circumstances.

When you're looking at a profile, look for ones that have candid photos of the person with others, doing things, with a pet, etc. If his profile looks like a modeling portfolio or he only has pictures of him alone in muscle shirts, do a reverse image search on those photos. Remember, if it looks too good to be true, it probably is. You may find photos on other people's social media pages, or those photos may actually be from a modeling portfolio—whatever the case, they're phony. Do not interact with anyone whose photos come up as not his or her own; the poster's intentions are not pure and he or she could be planning a sinister plot on your personal data.

201

Use the Dating Website or App Chat Until You Establish Trust

Almost all dating sites and apps have a chat feature that runs through the platform and allows you to send messages and start getting to know people you find online. You should stick to these communication channels exclusively until you feel you know whoever you're chatting with well enough to provide your phone number, address, or any other personal information. Dating sites are a business so they will have measures in place to monitor this messaging. If you suspect someone is using a fake profile or she's been acting inappropriately or asking you for personal details, you should report her so the dating site can keep her from getting to others as well.

While it may be tempting to just give out your phone number and text or have phone calls (because it's easier and you can do it throughout your day without logging into an online dating account) you should resist the urge. If the person you're interacting with is a fraud, then she may be looking for a way to get you texting so she can send your phone a virus and hack your personal data. While it may be less convenient, take the extra time to get to know someone in the secure chat before you ever give out your phone number.

Always Meet in Public Until You Get to Know Someone from an Online Dating Site

While you're still getting to know someone from an online dating site or app, when you meet up in person you should always meet in busy, public places. While it may be tempting if the person is charming and fun to be around, don't invite your date to your home or any other places personal to your life until you really know him and have a good idea of his intentions. Fraudsters know no bounds when it comes to trying to get the information they need to complete their con. While they're shameless, they can also be very charming and may be trying to get inside your home to lurk about and see what information they can find and steal.

Don't Leave Your Personal Items Unattended on a Date

When you decide to meet up for an in-person date with that special someone (you think) you've been talking to on a dating site or app, in addition to meeting somewhere public, you should also make sure you keep all your personal items close. Cons who peruse online dating apps are not above taking you on a date to steal your purse or wallet while your guard is down. If you need to go to the restroom or leave your seat for any reason, take your personal items with you. You may feel very comfortable with the person and think it's okay to have him watch your things for you for a couple of minutes, but that's exactly what he's counting on so he can steal tidbits of the personal information you carry around with you every day in your purse, wallet, or phone.

Remember:
Alcohol Clouds Judgment

It can be fun to unwind with a cocktail on a date (and it may help your nerves a bit if you're just meeting someone from your online dating endeavors in person for the first time) but remember that alcohol, even a little, can cloud your judgment. You should be very careful about how much alcohol you consume on dates (or even while chatting and meeting people online) because when you've been drinking, you'll be more off guard. You may give away too much personal information about yourself in what you say, or you might forget your phone on the way to the bathroom, or you might not give a second thought to having your date hold your purse while you climb into the cab. There are a lot of things that you could give away about yourself and your life to compromise your privacy if you have too much to drink, so use your best judgment and make sure that you keep your privacy (and yourself) safe.

205

Be Cautious of Urgent Requests for Help or Money on Dating Sites

Scammers use dating sites with a pretty sinister agenda in mind. They're preying on people who are actively trying to connect with others and will often begin coming to you with messages filled with urgency and drama soon after you've made an initial spark in your online dating interaction. Don't fall for these tricks. Remember, anything urgent like asking you for help or money in an online message is most likely a scam (particularly on dating sites when you've likely not even met this person in real life yet). If you begin receiving messages like this on the online dating platform you're using, don't engage any further. Delete and block that person and report their profile to the dating website immediately.

CHAPTER 7

Despite Your Best Intentions—Recovering from a Privacy Breach

If you spend any substantial time online or are a citizen of the world, you're likely going to experience some kind of privacy breach in your lifetime. Despite your best efforts, you may still get caught by a hacker, scammer, or other privacy villain who's just one step ahead of you. But this doesn't necessarily mean all is lost.

These privacy protection hacks will show you exactly how you can bounce back from a privacy invasion and be proactive in reclaiming your personal information quickly (while also setting yourself up for a more secure future in protecting your private details).

206

Know the Common Signs Your Accounts Have Been Hacked or Compromised

To notice when your privacy has been breached or an account has been hacked, you first need to understand the signs. If you know what you're looking for, then you'll be able to catch things much faster. In general, you should be watching for anything that seems different or "off." While sometimes it may just be a weird system glitch because software, mobile devices, and online accounts are not perfect, there are some things that should always give you concern, including:

- Slowed computer functionality or weird quirks surfacing
- Odd posts or messages that you didn't initiate in your social channels
- Ads suddenly taking over your screen
- Unrecognized charges on your bank statement
- Accounts you don't recognize on your credit report
- Weird email notifications
- An influx of spam mail, texts, or calls

Unfortunately, sometimes there will not be any signs when your privacy has been breached, at least not at first. If you ever notice something just isn't right on any of your devices, accounts, or in your personal life around you, then your privacy could be in jeopardy.

Change Your Passwords Immediately (*All* of Them)

The first thing you can do is to change your passwords. All of them. You should make a list of all the online accounts that you have (work, personal, social, banking, etc.) and then go through and change every password (remember: make passwords complex and random, and don't use the same one for all your accounts). Don't forget to change your Wi-Fi password, your mobile phone PINs, and then make sure everyone in your household changes all of their passwords too. Be thorough. This is your best defense against future breaches and will lock the criminals out (or at least give them a lot more hoops to jump through) and the more roadblocks you can put between them and your personal data, the better.

208

Verify You Were Impacted by a Privacy Breach

If your privacy was breached due to a hacker getting into the database of an account, platform, or institution you use, then after you've changed all your passwords you should follow the instructions provided by that organization to see if you were impacted in the breach. They should have a website you can visit or some type of notification process in place to let you know how much (and what) personal data of yours was compromised. Be diligent once you have these details, and make sure that you go through all the proper channels to recover your data and secure your accounts once more.

Alert Your Bank and Credit Card Companies

If your credit or debit card information has been involved in a large system breach with a retailer or other organization that has details of your past orders, then you should alert your credit card companies and your bank about the breach. They can put some protections in place to alert you to any spending or odd transactions and will work closely with you to make sure that no fraudulent charges can get through. In addition to calling or working via email with your credit card company and bank, you should also send them a written letter notifying them and outlining your expectations of how they should monitor your account. This will give you a paper trail and help you hold your banking institutions accountable as well.

Contact Credit Bureaus and Dispute Any Fraudulent Charges or Collections

If you've encountered any type of personal data breach, you should contact the major credit reporting bureaus and have them do some research to make sure that no new accounts have been opened up in your name. Check for any collections or derogatory remarks that may be on your credit report (as the result of someone else's actions). You can work with the bureaus to ensure that any incorrect data is removed. They can help you in making things right with any collections or credit companies who were also impacted as a result of your data getting into ill-intentioned hands.

Monitor Your Credit Carefully

While you should get into the habit of monitoring your credit regularly (as it's one of the first places you'll be clued into any potential privacy breaches), upon discovering you've been impacted by a data breach it's especially important to keep a close eye on your credit reports. Your credit report can work as an early warning system by alerting you if any new accounts are opened up in your name or if there are collections on bills that were never yours (but may have been set up in your name as a result of your data getting into the hands of cons). If you spot anything suspicious, look into it by contacting the credit agency that's filing a new account. If needed, you can enlist the help of the credit bureaus to help get rid of fraudulent accounts, but it's up to you to keep a close eye on your credit, so you notice if something odd appears and can take action to stop the fraud as quickly as possible.

212

Issue a Credit Freeze

If you know for certain that you've been impacted by a privacy breach and some of your personal information has already been used fraudulently, then you may need to take the more extreme action of freezing your credit. Doing so will ensure that no accounts whatsoever can be opened or created using any of your personal information. Whatever the crooks got hold of will be dead in their hands if you follow these steps:

- Contact each of the main credit bureaus.
- Connect with the fraud department and let them know your privacy has been breached and you'd like to freeze your credit.
- Pay a small fee (it's worth it) and wait until the privacy breach has run its course before you open up your credit capabilities once more.

Order New Credit and Debit Cards

If you're impacted in a data breach or have been victim to identity theft or any other type of hacking fraud, then it's in your best interest to order new credit and debit cards. Even if your banking or credit cards were not the source of your information leak, it's still important to protect yourself and your finances. It's not always evident exactly where your privacy breach has ended and if a large amount of your personal data has been exposed or compromised, then your financial information is probably part of what those criminals got their sticky fingers on. Visit your bank and take out enough cash to get by for a week or two, and then order all new cards. Don't forget to reset the passwords for any online accounts associated with those cards as well. Starting with a clean financial slate after a data breach is a great way to gain a bit of control and peace of mind, and it will help protect your finances by rendering your old debit and credit card numbers (that may very well be in the hands of crooks now) useless.

214

Identify Which Devices Were Impacted

The tricky part about having your data exposed in a privacy breach is that you may never know until things have already gone awry for you. But if you pay attention, you can spot some subtle changes in your devices that could signal they've been hacked as well. If you've suffered a privacy invasion, then you should carefully check all of your devices to make sure that they aren't operating slower. Be on the lookout for suspicious ads, texts, emails, or calls (especially if they start suddenly). Depending on what type of privacy breach has impacted you, it may also be a good idea to have your devices wiped to ensure that there are no lingering viruses or other gateways a hacker could use to return to your personal information again.

215

Regain Control
of Your Accounts

Whenever your personal data is compromised in one account, there's a good chance that data in other accounts you have online has been impacted as well. If a snoop on your Wi-Fi has gotten into one and you've noticed, then there may be other accounts infiltrated that you've yet to catch onto. As a good rule of thumb, any time an account you own is hacked, you should make the effort to reclaim your accounts by changing your passwords and amping up your privacy settings. Keep a close eye on all of your reclaimed accounts and make sure that you aren't seeing further fraudulent activity. For example, if a department store card you have has been stolen and is being used for purchases online, then you need to cancel that card and get a new one. But you also need to change your password in your online card account so that when you get your new card, the snoop doesn't simply log back in and start spending all over again on the new card that's linked to your account.

216

Delete Accounts or Start New Ones

If you're unable to reclaim your online accounts successfully after a security breach (or if you continue to experience issues with fraud, keep getting your social profile hacked, or still see unauthorized spending on your cards despite getting new ones) then you may have to delete the problematic accounts and start over fresh (or step away from social media altogether). Don't worry about how you'll ever find all your friends again or fret over having to set up new online accounts for your banking and credit cards. It's worth the effort to start with a clean slate if you're continually experiencing security issues. If the problem is consistent, it's time well spent to ensure that you're able to secure your private information and give the boot for good to the snoop who's constantly troubling you. It may take wiping out more than one account to get your data back in order and protected once more.

Don't Accept Help from Random Individuals or Companies after a Data Breach

However unbelievable it may seem, there are cons out there who use a fraudulent data breach perpetrated by someone else as their "in" to gather personal data for their data stealing. It takes a special kind of sneak thief to capitalize on someone who's already been victimized, with the intent of only further defrauding them, but sadly, such people are out there. If you've been impacted by a data breach and you begin receiving calls, emails, and texts from random (and seemingly well-meaning) individuals or companies offering their help, be very skeptical. There are cons who prey on this very situation—you've had your data breached and don't know exactly what to do—and will position themselves as experts who can help. However, what they're really trying to do is swindle you out of personal data or money; this at a time you're vulnerable and susceptible to their too-good-to-be-true offers. If the fraud you've experienced is more involved than changing passwords and updating your privacy settings, then you're probably best off consulting with a lawyer who can help point you in the correct direction.

Consider Cyberattack Insurance (but Do Your Research)

If you've fallen victim to privacy breaches in the past, or if you have a business online that you need to protect in addition to your personal privacy, then there are reputable cyberattack insurance companies who will help you protect yourself and your assets. But do your research before you dive into this.

- Don't interact with a cyberattack company that contacts you. You should be the one seeking them out.
- Vet the company thoroughly by reading reviews online and looking up their ratings. Read the good and the bad, paying close attention to the bad.
- Never give the company access to any of your accounts for an assessment. Make sure you have a contract in place and it's been reviewed by a lawyer.
- Remember, security systems are only ever as good as their last hack. Thieves are constantly innovating new ways to steal and ultimately, it's up to you to make sure your private data stays safe.

219

Don't Blame Yourself, but Learn from Your Experience

When your private information is exposed or your data is breached, it's natural to blame yourself and think about all the things you could have done to prevent this situation you're in now. Remember though, it wasn't you who misled or completely defrauded another person for your own gain or amusement. It's not your fault. It's true there may have been some things that you did (or didn't do) that made it easier for a con to get to your data. Don't waste time blaming yourself; just take those thoughts about all the things you could have done differently to avoid a privacy breach and channel them into action. Do them now and learn from your experience so you're more savvy and careful about your privacy and what it truly takes to keep it protected from cons, hackers, and busybodies.

220

Share Your Story to Help Others Protect Their Privacy

Privacy invasions are scary and they can do a lot of damage to your life that you'd never wish upon others. As you're learning more about how to protect your privacy, online and offline, don't keep your tips and insights to yourself! Share what you are learning or have learned through a personal experience with being hacked, having your data mined, or being a victim of fraud. Sharing your experience and what you've learned opens up the conversation about privacy with your friends and family. It helps keep everyone aware and encourages an open dialogue about how we can all protect our private information and keep it out of the hands of cons who use everyday channels and loopholes some people may never think of to gain access and commit fraud against strangers. The more loopholes you can close, the more channels you can close, and the more hoops you can put between criminals and your personal data, the better off you'll be. That's a message worth sharing, so share your story and experience, and listen when others do the same.

Make Your Privacy a Priority

Protecting your privacy is important, so it should be treated as a priority in your life. Don't be tempted to trade convenience for security by getting complacent about keeping your privacy intact online, offline, and everywhere in-between. Don't procrastinate and think that you'll change those passwords later or you'll run your security update after you check your email. Make your privacy a priority now.

Conclusion

The truth is that innovation, while driving progress, will always open loopholes that those with evil intentions will exploit by trying to gain access to your personal or private information.

We can't reprogram human nature, but what we can do is use the privacy protection hacks you've learned by reading this book to be aware and stay diligent against the privacy risks that exist as a reality in today's world. You expect huge companies, technology providers, and online social networks and retailers to protect your personal data, and for the most part they do, but protecting your privacy, both online and offline, means that you have to play an active role in ensuring you're not doing anything that makes it easier for your personal data to be compromised. This involves training yourself to think about your personal information from a different perspective.

The perspective of a swindler who would want to get his sticky fingers near your private data.

The perspective of a clever hacker who looks for loopholes, backdoors, or system weaknesses he can use to move undetected from the outside, in.

Your own perspective of what data is safe to share (and what is not).

The tips and privacy protection hacks in this book will help you notice your privacy-risking behaviors, patterns, and routines, and understand the measures you can take to be personally responsible for your own privacy (because a great deal of it *is* within your control)!

Stay proactive and diligent. You're ultimately the one in charge of all the personal data that defines you and that's always worth protecting.

References

"21 Tips, Tricks, and Shortcuts to Help Your Stay Anonymous Online." www.theguardian.com/technology/2015/mar/06/ tips-tricks-anonymous-privacy [Accessed 6 July 2018]

"Enable BitLocker on USB Flash Drives to Protect Data." https://technet.microsoft.com/en-us/library/ff404223.aspx [Accessed 13 July 2018]

"How Can I Secure My FitBit Account and Data?" https://help.fitbit .com/articles/en_US/Help_article/1758 [Accessed 1 July 2018]

"How to Keep Your Personal Information Secure." www.consumer .ftc.gov/articles/0272-how-keep-your-personal-information-secure [Accessed 26 July 2018]

"How to Protect Your Privacy on Your Smart Home Devices." https://lifehacker.com/how-to-protect-your-privacy-on-your-smart- home-devices-1823181500 [Accessed 11 June 2018]

"How to Secure Your (Easily Hackable) Smart Home." www .tomsguide.com/us/secure-smart-home-how-to,news-19380 .html [Accessed 1 July 2018]

"3 Things You Should Know About Europe's Sweeping New Data Privacy Law." www.npr.org/sections/alltechconsidered/ 2018/05/24/613983268/a-cheat-sheet-on-europe-s-sweeping- privacy-law [Accessed 9 September 2018]

"Facebook and Other Firms Have a Ton of Data on You. Here's How to Limit That." www.npr.org/2018/04/12/601881444/ facebook-and-other-firms-have-a-ton-of-data-on-you-heres-how- to-limit-that [Accessed 9 September 2018]

"2017 Was the Year of the Hacks. 2018 Probably Won't Be Better." www.huffingtonpost.com/entry/data-breach-hacks_us_5a3a7f56e 4b025f99e13cdbe [Accessed 9 September 2018]

"Let's Retire the Phrase 'Privacy Policy.'" www.nytimes.com/2018/08/20/opinion/20Turow.html?rref=collection%2Ftimestop ic%2FOnline%20Privacy%20Regulation&action=click&content Collection=timestopics&region=stream&module=stream_ unit&version=latest&contentPlacement=3&pgtype=collection [Accessed 9 September 2018]

"The Illusion of Online Privacy." www.usnews.com/news/articles/2015/08/25/the-illusion-of-online-privacy [Accessed 21 July 2018]

"The Risk of Third-Party App Stores." https://us.norton.com/internetsecurity-mobile-the-risks-of-third-party-app-stores.html [Accessed 21 July 2018]

"What Is a Firewall?" www.cisco.com/c/en/us/products/security/firewalls/what-is-a-firewall.html [Accessed 9 September 2018]

Index

A

Addresses (email). *See* Email(s)
Addresses (street/other)
    keeping out of online photos or ads, 182, 215
    kids' possessions and, 63, 71. *See also* Children, privacy of
    luggage tags and, 71
    new checks sent to alternate address, 29
    using multiple strategically, 28, 29
Addresses (web), HTTPS vs. HTTP, 131. *See also* Internet and online privacy/safety
Attachments, to not open, 202

B

Baby monitor, privacy tips, 43, 44
Birthday date precautions, 53
Bluetooth, 102, 125
Breaches, news reports about, 58
Breaches, recovering from, 227–43
    about: overview of, 227
    alerting bank and credit card companies, 231
    changing passwords immediately, 229. *See also* Passwords
    cons preying on victims after breach, 239
    contacting credit bureaus, 232
    cyberattack insurance and, 240
    deleting accounts, 238
    help after breach (precaution), 239
    identifying devices impacted, 236
    issuing credit freeze, 234
    learning from experience, 241
    making privacy a priority, 243
    monitoring credit carefully, 233
    ordering new credit and debit cards, 235
    preventing repeat occurrences, 241, 245
    regaining control of accounts, 237
    sharing story to help others, 242
    signs of having been hacked/compromised, 228
    starting new accounts, 238
    verifying impact of privacy breach, 230

C

Cameras and photos. *See* Mobile devices, privacy and; Photos
Catfishing ploys on dating sites, 221
Cell phones. *See* Mobile devices, privacy and
Children, privacy of, 60–88
    about: overview of, 60
    advocating at school, 72
    app review and guidelines, 67, 68
    code word or gesture for privacy cue, 66
    disabling location settings, 70
    empowerment child to say "No," 64
    family computer location and, 87
    "friends" precautions, 80–81
    gaming precautions, 84–86
    house key/home security tips, 76
    online photos and, 78, 82
    online risks, 67–70, 77–86
    open dialogue policy on privacy concerns, 74, 79, 88
    overseeing/monitoring what goes on, 61, 65, 67, 70, 73, 84, 87
    passwords protections, 75
    PIN number protection and, 65
    protecting birth details/identity of children, 180
    publicly-seen items (backpacks/luggage, jackets, etc.) and, 63, 71
    range of solutions, 61

O

About the Author

Jeni Rogers is a freelance writer and consultant specializing in B2B software and technology business sectors and privacy and security industries. Her work appears regularly on leading business blogs where she is a featured guest expert.

Improve Your Life—
One Hack at a Time!

Life Hacks
(lĭf, hăks) noun.

College Hacks
(kä-lĭj, hăks) noun.

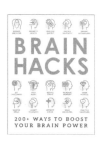

BRAIN
HACKS

200+ WAYS TO BOOST
YOUR BRAIN POWER

LONGWOOD PUBLIC LIBRARY
800 Middle Country Road
Middle Island, NY 11953
(631) 924-6400
longwoodlibrary.org

LIBRARY HOURS

Monday-Friday	9:30 a.m. - 9:00 p.m.
Saturday	9:30 a.m. - 5:00 p.m.
Sunday (Sept-June)	1:00 p.m. - 5:00 p.m.